SALT LAKE COUNTY LIBRARY SYSTEM
purchased at Public Sale

ALL-IN-ALL

*George Eliot, from a portrait painted
by D'Albert Durade*

ALL-IN-ALL

A Biography of George Eliot

LouAnn Gaeddert

[George Eliot] showed, from the earliest years, the trait
that was most marked in her all through life, namely, the
absolute need of some one person who should be all-in-
all to her, and to whom she should be all-in-all.

—John Cross

E. P. Dutton & Co., Inc.   New York

61801

SALT LAKE
COUNTY
LIBRARY SYSTEM

EXTENSION

For my niece, Anne

Copyright © 1976 by LouAnn Gaeddert

All rights reserved. No part of this publication may be
reproduced or transmitted in any form or by any means,
electronic or mechanical, including photocopy, recording,
or any information storage and retrieval system now
known or to be invented, without permission in writing
from the publisher, except by a reviewer who wishes to
quote brief passages in connection with a review written
for inclusion in a magazine, newspaper, or broadcast.

Library of Congress Cataloging in Publication Data

Gaeddert, LouAnn Bigge   All-in-all

SUMMARY: A biography of Marian Evans, a Victorian
writer who adopted a male pen name to
preserve her privacy.

1. Eliot, George, pseud., i.e. Marian Evans, afterwards
Cross, 1819–1880—Biography—Juvenile literature.
[1. Eliot, George, pseud., i.e. Marian Evans, afterwards
Cross, 1819–1880. 2. Authors, English]   I. Title.
PR4681.G3   823'.8   [B]   [92]   76–14791   ISBN 0–525–25440–4

Published simultaneously in Canada by Clarke,
Irwin & Company Limited, Toronto and Vancouver

Editor: Ann Durell
Designer: Meri Shardin
Printed in the U.S.A.   First Edition
10 9 8 7 6 5 4 3 2 1

❧ CONTENTS ❧

BOOK I

Mary Ann

~ 1 ~

MARY ANN EVANS was being driven from her home. She was packing her comb and brush into the top of her last bag, and still she found it difficult to believe that her father could cast her out. She had been his favorite child. "The little wench," he had called her.

Now, because she refused to participate in his religion, he had put their house on the market and was making plans to move to a small cottage where there would be no room for her. Mary Ann would be forced to teach in a school to earn enough for the bare essentials of life.

It was harsh and unnecessary. They should have been able to discuss their differences, but they were two strong-minded individuals. She had tried to explain her views in a long letter to him, silly as it seemed to write to someone she saw every morning at breakfast. The letter had been useless. Mr. Evans was an unquestioning supporter of the established Church of England. Her refusal to attend church with him was such a disgrace that he felt it impossible to hold his head up and pass the collection plate during Sunday services. He had issued an ultimatum. She could either adopt Christian views and attend church with him or get out. It was as simple as that in his eyes. It was a matter of principle in hers. Still, she loved her father and she knew that he loved her.

A carpenter by trade, Robert Evans had risen to the highly responsible position of agent of the Arbury estate, owned by the titled Newdigate family. The estate in the midlands of England consisted of seven thousand acres of farms, woodland, coal mines, a canal, and a maze of roads. He had managed them all, plus several other estates in the area, for many years—until his recent retirement.

He was old for a father, nearly as old as the grandfathers of some of her friends. She was his youngest child and her birth had been noted in his diary in his usual precise way. "Nov. 22, 1819.—Mary Ann Evans was born at Arbury Farm at five o'clock this morning." He had four other children. A son and daughter had been born to his first wife, who had later died. Chrissey, born in 1814, and Isaac, born in 1816, were, like Mary Ann, the children of his second wife.

Mary Ann could not remember when her father's hair had not been gray, but he was a man of great distinction to whom gray hair seemed appropriate. As a little girl she had felt that she could draw attention to her own merits just by mentioning that she was the daughter of Robert Evans. Neighbors still told stories of his physical strength. Once two laborers were waiting idly in a field for a third man to come to help them move a very long, heavy ladder from one haystack to another. Mr. Evans came by and saw his men doing nothing. He braced himself, slowly lifted the ladder, and carried it by himself. He was also known for his astuteness. He could look at a tree and tell how many board feet it would yield. He was often asked to value land.

Mary Ann had taken pride in all his accomplishments, but more important to her were his sympathy and love. He often took her with him when he rode about the estate. He listened to her stories and bragged about her intelligence. All her life Mary Ann needed one person who would be all-in-all to her and to whom she would be all-in-all. At times during her childhood that person was her father.

Her last bag was packed and closed. She went downstairs to where her father was waiting to hand her into the carriage. He kissed her on the forehead. If only he would take her in his arms and call her his little wench just once more.

"Good-bye, Father," she whispered.

"Good-bye, Mary Ann."

That was all. No last minute pleading. No warm endearments. Just resignation. The servant lifted the reins and the horse trotted away. Mary Ann looked back at her father, standing stooped and old in front of their house. Then she buried her face in her hands and wept.

As the carriage rolled along peaceful country lanes, Mary Ann's tears subsided. She wrapped herself more snugly in the carriage robe and began to look around her. The March winds were cold, but they carried the promise of spring. Green shoots peeked through the brown stubble of the fields. Buds were swelling on some of the trees. The land was so flat that she could see for miles in every direction. Visitors described this country around Coventry as dull. It was beautiful to Mary Ann. In the future she would travel to the romantic cities of Europe, she would live in the center of the cultural excitement of London, but she would return to the English countryside for solace.

Now she was returning to Griff House. Robert Evans had moved his family into the vine-covered, red-brick house when Mary Ann was just four months old. She had lived there until her father had relinquished his house, his farm, and his professional responsibilities to his son Isaac.

Isaac. How she had loved Isaac! He had been her all-in-all person through her earliest years. She would be a visitor at Griff now, living with him and his wife until she could find a teaching position, but it would be a welcome respite. She could say good-bye to her girlhood and gather strength to meet the responsibilities of adulthood.

In the distance she heard the thundering of horses' hooves. The driver pulled the carriage to a stop at the side of the road to make room for the stagecoach drawn by four great horses. Mary Ann smiled. Twice a day, every pleasant day, when she and Isaac were little, they had run to the front gate at Griff to watch the stage. On rainy days they had watched from the attic window. The stage was their link with the outside world.

Isaac and Mary Ann had no other children to play with. Chrissey was not only older than they, she was also too much the little lady to be interested in their games. The two younger Evans children, therefore, depended on one another for their daily joy. They roamed the fields together. They watched barges in the canal carrying coal from the mines to the market. They fished in the round pond behind their house, coming home covered with mud to face their disgrace together. On rainy days they played in the attic.

Even now Mary Ann was convinced that there never was such a brother as the little boy Isaac—until the day he was given a pony. On that day he had begun to grow away from her. She had tried to run after him, but no little girl could compete with a pony.

The carriage stopped in front of her beloved Griff House. Isaac and his wife were waiting to welcome her. She was home, if only for a visit.

❧ 2 ❧

"I WILL NEVER BELIEVE that our youngest days are our happiest," the adult Mary Ann wrote. "Childhood is only the beautiful and happy time in contemplation and retrospect: to the child it is full of deep sorrows, the meaning of which is unknown. Witness colic and whooping-cough and dread of ghosts, to say nothing of hell and Satan, and an offended Deity in the sky who was angry when I wanted too much plumcake."

Christiana Pearson Evans, Mary Ann's mother, was probably the cause of much of her daughter's sorrow. One of four daughters of a small landowner, she had not married until her mid-twenties, late in an age when marriage was the *only* vocation for a woman. Her husband was fifteen years her senior, a widower with two children, and beneath her socially. It may, therefore, have been a marriage of convenience rather than love.

Within six years of her marriage, Mrs. Evans had given birth to three children. She then seemed determined to rid the house of children as quickly as possible. Her stepson, Robert, was sent to manage a distant estate at the age of seventeen or eighteen. His sister, Fanny, no more than fifteen years old, was sent with him to act as his housekeeper. Her own children were sent to boarding school, Mary Ann at the incredibly young age of five. It may be said on Mrs. Evans' behalf that she was ill following the birth of her last child, exactly how ill we do not know.

Nothing in Mary Ann's letters or books gives a solid clue to her relationship with her mother. It appears that Mrs. Evans preferred both Chrissey and Isaac to her youngest child. Mary Ann may never have experienced intense maternal love. She may have tried to find a substitute for that love in her devotion to her brother and her father. Several of the heroines of her novels were motherless, and yet a few of the minor characters in her books were devoted mothers and entirely believable.

Some aspects of Mary Ann's childhood read like an open book entitled *The Mill on the Floss.* This tragic novel is about a brother and sister, Maggie and Tom Tulliver. The plot is pure fabrication, but the characters of the brother and sister are drawn directly from the author's memory of herself and Isaac. And drawn extraordinarily well. Many critics consider the early chapters of the book to contain the most nearly perfect word portrait of childhood ever written. It is completely stripped of sentimentality.

Although Mrs. Tulliver bears no relationship to Mrs. Evans, the three maternal aunts—Aunt Glegg, Aunt Pullet, and Aunt Deane— were surely drawn directly from Mrs. Evans' three sisters. These good ladies were devoted to the sacred principle of doing things—from preparing tea to burying the dead—right. They were also devoted to family solidarity. There is no older sister in *The Mill,* but cousin Lucy Deane bore some resemblance to placid, pretty Chrissey. The following excerpts from *The Mill on the Floss* reveal the characters of Mary Ann and Isaac and demonstrate Mary Ann's warm relationship to her father. (It is also an example of George Eliot's style and wit.) The aunts and their husbands have come to dinner to discuss Mr. Tulliver's plans for his son's education.

§   . . . [Maggie] and Tom came in from the garden with their father and their uncle Glegg. Maggie had thrown her bonnett off very carelessly, and coming in with her hair rough as well as out of curl, rushed at once to Lucy, who was standing by her mother's knee. Certainly the contrast between the cousins was conspicuous, and to superficial eyes was very much to the disadvantage of Maggie, though a connoisseur might have seen "points" in her which had a higher promise for maturity than Lucy's natty completeness. It was like the contrast between a rough, dark, overgrown puppy and a white kitten. . . . Maggie always looked at Lucy with delight. She was fond of fancying a world where the people never got any larger than children of their own age, and she made the queen of it just like Lucy, with a little crown on her head and a little sceptre in her hand . . . only the queen was Maggie herself in Lucy's form.

"Oh Lucy," she burst out after kissing her, "you'll stay with Tom and me, won't you? Oh, kiss her, Tom."

Tom too had come up to Lucy, but he was not going to kiss her—no; he came up to her with Maggie because it seemed easier, on the whole, than saying, "How do you do?" to all those aunts and uncles; he stood looking at nothing in particular, with the blushing, awkward air and semi-smile which are common to shy boys when in company—very much as if they had come into the world by mistake and found it in a degree of undress that was quite embarrassing.

"Heyday!" said aunt Glegg with loud emphasis. "Do little boys and gells come into a room without taking notice o' their uncles and aunts? That wasn't the way when *I* was a little gell."

"Go and speak to your aunts and uncles, my dears," said Mrs. Tulliver, looking anxious and melancholy. She wanted to whisper to Maggie a command to go and have her hair brushed.

"Well, and how do you do? And I hope you're good children, are you?" said aunt Glegg in the same loud emphatic way as she took their hands, hurting them with her large rings and kissing their cheeks much against their desire. "Look up, Tom, look up. Boys as go to boarding schools should hold their heads up. Look at me now." Tom declined that pleasure apparently, for he tried to draw his hand away. "Put your hair behind your ears, Maggie, and keep your frock on your shoulder."

Aunt Glegg always spoke to them in this loud emphatic way, as if she considered them deaf or perhaps rather idiotic; it was a means, she thought, of making them feel that they were accountable creatures, and might be a salutary check on naughty tendencies. . . .

"Well, my dears," said aunt Pullet in a compassionate voice, "you grow wonderful fast. I doubt they'll outgrow their strength," she added, looking over their heads with a melancholy expression at their mother. "I think the gell has too much hair. I'd have it thinned and cut shorter, sister, if I was you; it isn't good for her health. It's that as makes her skin so brown. I shouldn't wonder. Don't you think so, sister Deane?"

"I can't say, I'm sure, sister," said Mrs. Deane, shutting her lips close again and looking at Maggie with a critical eye.

"No, no," said Mr. Tulliver, "the child's healthy enough— there's nothing ails her. There's red wheat as well as white, for that matter, and some like the dark grain best. But it 'ud be well if Bessy 'ud have the child's hair cut, so as it 'ud lie smooth."

A dreadful resolve was gathering in Maggie's breast. . . .

"Maggie," said Mrs. Tulliver, beckoning Maggie to her and whispering in her ear . . . "go and get your hair brushed—do, for shame. I told you not to come in without going to Martha first; you know I did."

"Tom, come out with me," whispered Maggie, pulling his sleeve as she passed him; and Tom followed willingly enough.

"Come upstairs with me, Tom," she whispered when they were outside the door. "There's something I want to do before dinner."

"There's no time to play at anything before dinner," said Tom, whose imagination was impatient of any intermediate prospect.

"Oh, yes, there is time for this—*do* come, Tom."

Tom followed Maggie upstairs into her mother's room and saw her go at once to a drawer, from which she took out a large pair of scissors.

"What are they for, Maggie?" said Tom, feeling his curiosity awakened.

Maggie answered by seizing her front locks and cutting them straight across the middle of her forehead.

"Oh, my buttons, Maggie, you'll catch it!" exclaimed Tom. "You'd better not cut any more off."

Snip! went the great scissors again while Tom was speaking; and he couldn't help feeling it was rather good fun; Maggie would look so queer.

"Here, Tom, cut it behind for me," said Maggie, excited by her own daring and anxious to finish the deed.

"You'll catch it, you know," said Tom, nodding his head in an admonitory manner and hesitating a little as he took the scissors.

"Never mind—make haste!" said Maggie, giving a little stamp with her foot. Her cheeks were quite flushed.

The black locks were so thick—nothing could be more tempting to a lad who had already tasted the forbidden pleasure of cutting the pony's mane. I speak to those who know the satisfaction of making a pair of shears meet through a duly resisting mass of hair. One delicious grinding snip and then another and another, and the hinder-locks fell heavily on the floor, and Maggie stood cropped in a jagged, uneven manner, but with a sense of clearness and freedom, as if she had emerged from a wood into the open plain.

"Oh, Maggie," said Tom, jumping round her and slapping his knees as he laughed. "Oh, my buttons, what a queer thing you look! Look at yourself in the glass—you look like the idiot we throw our nut-shells to at school."

Maggie felt an unexpected pang. She had thought beforehand chiefly of her own deliverance from her teasing hair and teasing remarks about it, and something also of the triumph she should have over her mother and her aunts by this very decided course of action: she didn't want her hair to look pretty—that was out of the question—she only wanted people to think her a clever little girl and not to find fault with her. But now, when Tom began to laugh at her and say she was like the idiot, the affair had quite a new aspect. She looked in the glass, and still Tom laughed and clapped his hands, and Maggie's flushed cheeks began to pale, and her lips to tremble a little.

"Oh, Maggie, you'll have to go down to dinner directly," said Tom. "Oh, my!"

"Don't laugh at me, Tom," said Maggie in a passionate tone, with an outburst of angry tears, stamping, and giving him a push.

"Now, then, spitfire!" said Tom. "What did you cut it off for, then? I shall go down; I can smell the dinner going in."

He hurried downstairs and left poor Maggie to that bitter sense of the irrevocable which was almost an everyday experience of her small soul. She could see clearly enough, now the thing was done, that it was very foolish and that she would have to hear and think more about her hair than ever, for Maggie rushed to her deeds with passionate impulse and then saw not only their conse- quences but what would have happened if they had not been done. . . . Tom never did the same sort of foolish things as Maggie, having a wonderful instinctive discernment of what would turn to his advantage or disadvantage; and so it happened that his mother hardly ever called him naughty. . . .

"Maggie, you little silly," said Tom, peeping into the room ten minutes after, "why don't you come and have your dinner? There's lots o' goodies, and mother says you're to come. What are you crying for, you little spooney?"

Oh, it was dreadful! Tom was so hard and unconcerned; if *he* had been crying on the floor, Maggie would have cried too. And there was the dinner, so nice; and she was *so* hungry. It was very bitter.

But Tom was not altogether hard. He was not inclined to cry, and did not feel that Maggie's grief spoiled his prospect of the sweets; but he went and put his head near her and said in a lower, comforting tone, "Won't you come, then, Maggie? Shall I bring you a bit o' pudding when I've had mine? And a custard and things?"

"Ye-e-es," said Maggie, beginning to feel life a little more tolerable.

"Very well," said Tom, going away. But he turned again at the door and said, "But you'd better come, you know. There's the dessert—nuts, you know—and cowslip wine."

Maggie's tears had ceased, and she looked reflective as Tom left her. His good nature had taken off the keenest edge of her suffering, and nuts with cowslip wine began to assert their legitimate influence.

Slowly she rose from amongst her scattered locks, and slowly she made her way downstairs. . . .

Mrs. Tulliver gave a little scream as she saw her, and felt such a "turn" that she dropped the large gravy-spoon into the dish, with the most serious results to the tablecloth. . . .

Mrs. Tulliver's scream made all eyes turn towards the same point as her own, and Maggie's cheeks and ears began to burn, while uncle Glegg, a kind-looking, white-haired old gentleman, said, "Heyday! What little gell's this—why, I don't know her. . . ."

"Why, she's gone and cut her hair herself," said Mr. Tulliver in an undertone to Mr. Deane, laughing with much enjoyment. "Did you ever know such a little hussy as it is?"

"Why, little miss, you've made yourself look very funny," said uncle Pullet, and perhaps he never in his life made an observation which was felt to be so lacerating.

"Fie, for shame!" said aunt Glegg in her loudest, severest tone of reproof. "Little gells as cut their own hair should be whipped and fed on bread and water, not come and sit down with their aunts and uncles."

"Aye, aye," said uncle Glegg, meaning to give a playful turn to this denunciation, "she must be sent to jail, I think, and they'll cut the rest of her hair off there and make it all even."

"She's more like a Gypsy nor ever," said aunt Pullet in a pitying tone; "it's very bad luck, sister, as the gell should be so brown—the boy's fair enough. I doubt it'll stand in her way i' life to be so brown."

"She's a naughty child, as'll break her mother's heart," said Mrs. Tulliver, with the tears in her eyes.

Maggie seemed to be listening to a chorus of reproach and derision. Her first flush came from anger, which gave her a transient power of defiance, and Tom thought she was braving it out, supported by the recent appearance of the pudding and custard. Under this impression he whispered, "Oh my! Maggie, I told you you'd catch it." He meant to be friendly, but Maggie felt convinced that Tom was rejoicing in her ignominy. Her feeble power of defiance left her in an instant, her heart swelled, and getting up from her chair, she ran to her father, hid her face on his shoulder, and burst out into loud sobbing.

"Come, come, my wench," said her father soothingly, putting his arm around her, "never mind; you was i' the right to cut it off if it plagued you, give over crying: father'll take your part."

Delicious words of tenderness! Maggie never forgot any of these moments when her father "took her part". . . .

With the dessert there came entire deliverance for Maggie, for the children were told they might have their nuts and wine in the summer-house, since the day was so mild, and they scampered out among the budding bushes of the garden with the alacrity of small animals getting from under a burning glass. . . . §

Maggie Tulliver wanted people to "think her a very clever little girl." So did Mary Ann Evans. She later recalled an incident which took place when she was four years old. In an effort to impress the servants with her great cleverness, she seated herself at the piano one day and, without knowing a note of music, pounded out what she then thought was a very convincing piano recital.

MARY ANN'S formal education began even before she was sent away to school. She and Isaac attended a small school which a Mrs. Moore ran in her own home for very young children. It was located just outside the gates of Griff. Mary Ann was reportedly slow to learn to read. Isaac later attributed this to her greater interest in play, hardly unusual for a three- or four-year-old. The child, who was to become one of the great intellectuals of her age, found her joy in her brother and in his activities—running through the fields, playing in the mud, fishing. There is no indication that Isaac ever became a scholar.

When she was five, she was sent away to Miss Lathom's, a school Chrissey was already attending. Isaac was also sent to boarding school that year, but he was eight, a more common age to be sent from home. Although Miss Lathom's was but two miles from Griff, it might just as well have been twenty. Mary Ann and Chrissey only came home when they were ill, or for long holidays and for an occasional Saturday.

In later years Mary Ann could remember little about Miss Lathom's except two sensations which plagued her for the rest of her life. One was an unusual susceptibility to cold. She was so much smaller than the other girls at school that she could not get near the narrow fireplace. The other was night terrors. She reported being happy enough during the day, but at night "all her soul became a quivering fear."

But she did learn to read at Miss Lathom's, the beginning of her lifelong love affair with books. In the last year of her life she gave her husband a little volume entitled *The Linnet's Life.* It bore the following inscription: "This little book is the first present I ever remember having received from my father. Let any one who thinks of me with some tenderness after I am dead take care of this book for my sake. It made me very happy when I held it in my little hands, and read it over and over again; and thought the pictures beautiful, especially the one where the linnet is feeding her young."

She also read *Aesop's Fables* and a *Joe Miller Jest Book.* She loved to astonish her family with stories from these books. Another book that was in her home was Daniel Defoe's *History of the Devil,* which may have contributed to her night terrors.

When she was eight or nine a neighbor lent a copy of Sir Walter Scott's *Waverley* to Chrissey. Mary Ann started to read the novel but it was returned to its owner before she could finish it. With the fascinating book gone, she began to write down the story as far as she read it. Her parents discovered what she was doing and asked for the book back again so that Mary Ann could finish it. This marked the beginning of a lifelong enthusiasm for Scott.

When Mary Ann was nine she and Chrissey were sent to a larger boarding school, Mrs. Wallington's in Nuneaton. Mary Ann had become a loner, living in the world of books and her imagination. She seemed to have made no close friends of her own age. One woman reported seeing her sitting alone at a children's party.

"My dear, you do not seem happy; are you enjoying yourself?" the woman asked.

"No, I am not," Mary Ann replied. "I don't like to play with children. I like to talk to grown-up people."

Only one person seems to have penetrated the child's wall of self-sufficiency during her years at Mrs. Wallington's. That was a teacher at the school, Maria Lewis, a squint-eyed young Irish woman. She took an immediate and lasting interest in the homely child. Miss Lewis was a disciple of Evangelicalism, a religious movement based on Bible reading, self-improvement, and good works. Mary Ann embraced her teacher's faith with fervor, reading the Bible through several times. She also began to show signs of remarkable intellectual ability and in four years mastered everything the school had to offer.

At home on holidays she and Isaac had found a new common pleasure, performing charades for the entertainment of their family. At home, too, she was beginning to be recognized as a child with unusual abilities.

Chrissey's education apparently ended after four years at Mrs. Wallington's, but Mary Ann was sent on to an excellent school in Coventry. The school was run by two sisters, Mary and Rebecca Franklin, the daughters of a Baptist minister. They were well qualified to teach and surprisingly liberal. They encouraged their students to read widely, even the novels which were often despised as frivolous time-wasters. They also employed part-time instructors in music and foreign languages.

Mary Ann was their prize pupil. She developed a great interest in music, and it was not long before the music master confessed that he had nothing more to teach her. She was often called to the parlor to play the piano for guests. A shy girl, she would perform well and then rush to her room to weep.

She was also said to have excelled in English composition. The following is a paragraph from an essay entitled "Affectation and Conceit" found in a notebook which has survived from her school days. The punctuation is Mary Ann's own.

§ . . . so conscious are [conceited women] of the power of their personal attractions that in youth they do not generally as yet, exert themselves to affect much beyond a fancied superiority: They are conceited not affected but when that youth departs alas how often do we find the conceited woman one mass of nothing but affectation, real genuine affectation—She is so used to admiration that she finds it impossible to live without it, and as the drunkard turns to his wine to drown his cares, she the former beauty, finding all that before naturally attracted gone, flies to artificial means, in order she vainly hopes and believes to secure still her usual need of adulation—She affects a youthful walk, & a youthful manner, upon all occasions, and at the age of fifty may often be seen clothed in the girlish fashion of sixteen totally forgetting that her once rounded neck and shoulders which at the latter age, were properly uncovered, are now pointed & scraggy and would be much better hidden from sight by a more matronly habiliment. . . . §

Also included in the notebook is her first known fiction, the opening chapters of a wildly romantic novel in which the hero's first words are these:

§ "Well done my brave and trusty Ronald said he addressing his horse & patting him, thou hast served me this day better than thou hast ever before done, though never yet, hast thou been lacking in thy service to thy master, but I will urge thee no more. Now thy trusty feet have brought me where I had scarcely ever dared hope I might again come—Welcome welcome to my eyes the scene of my happiest days, and yet in what a manner have I returned to thee, an outcast from society I used to shine in and alien from my family a deserter, and a regicide; as he pronounced the last word a bitter smile curled his lip and dashing the tear from his eye, in a moment resumed his former reckless demeanor he crossed the bridge. . . ." §

Her friendship with Miss Lewis continued. The teacher visited in the Evans home, and they probably corresponded with one another. Mary Ann, however, made few new friends. As one of her schoolmates at Franklin School explained, "Her schoolfellows loved her as much as they could venture to love one whom they felt to be so immeasurably superior to themselves."

In the meantime she was becoming increasingly pious. She led prayer groups and began to neglect her personal appearance to display her greater concern for the state of her soul.

~ 4 ~

THE TERM ending at Christmastime 1835 was Mary Ann's last term of formal schooling. She had just passed her sixteenth birthday.

That Christmas Mrs. Evans was critically ill. Shortly after Christmas Mr. Evans, too, became ill. Mary Ann described conditions at home in a letter to Miss Lewis dated January 6, 1836:

> . . . We dare not hope that there will be a permanent improvement [in Mother's health]. Our anxieties on my mother's account though so great, have been since Thursday almost lost sight of in the more sudden, and consequently more severe, trial which we have been called on to endure in the alarming illness of my dear father. For four days we had no cessation of our anxiety; but I am thankful to say that he is now considered out of danger, though very much reduced by frequent bleeding and very powerful medicines.

Mr. Evans survived both the illness and the bleeding. A common medical practice of the day, bleeding involved opening veins to remove blood and its impurities.

All three of the Evans children were living at home when Mrs. Evans died on February 3.

For a time Mary Ann and Chrissey shared the housekeeping duties at Griff. Then in the spring of the following year, 1837, Chrissey married Dr. Edward Clarke. On Chrissey's wedding day, Isaac and Mary Ann sat down and had a good cry together. Mary Ann's relationship with her sister is more easily defined than her relationship with her mother. The sisters had little in common—except deep affection.

After Chrissey's marriage the sole responsibility of household management fell on seventeen-year-old Mary Ann. She had servants to help her, but the burdens of keeping house in those days can hardly be imagined today. There were fires to lay in every room. Laundry was laborious. The kitchen was necessarily the scene of endless activity. Mary Ann did what was required, probably even did it well. She did not always do it cheerfully. In letters written at that time she complained of cooking and entertaining as matters "nauseating to me."

"I write with a very tremulous hand . . . attributable to a very mighty cause—no other than the boiling of currant jelly! I have had much of this kind of occupation lately, and I grieve to say I have not gone through it so cheerfully as the character of a Christian who professes to do all . . . as the Lord demands," she wrote to Miss Lewis.

She had one other regular correspondent at this time, Patty Jackson, a girl her own age whom she had met at Franklin School. To Patty she wrote, "Pity the sorrows of a poor young housekeeper and determine to make the very best of your present freedom therefrom."

Busy as she was with her hateful household duties, she was determined to continue to grow intellectually. Tutors came to Griff to instruct her in music, Italian, and German. Her interest in learning was remarkable; even more remarkable was her father's support of that interest. Robert Evans himself had little formal schooling. His daughter had received a superior education. Girls of her day and class were taught to read, write, and do simple arithmetic. They might also be exposed to such graceful arts as French, music, and painting. Nothing more was necessary for a young lady whose only goal in life must be to make a "good marriage"—that is, to marry a man whose social position and finances were better than her own. Yet there is no record of any criticism of the money and time spent on Mary Ann's education.

Perhaps Robert Evans was only being realistic. He was growing old and he had no fortune to leave his daughter. She had no beauty with which to snare a husband. She would probably have to teach, and the better her education, the better position she could hope to find. On the other hand, he may have cooperated with her desire to study simply because he took pride in her ability.

Robert Evans may also have hoped that music and languages would divert her mind from the dark channels of piety that were making her an uncomfortable person to live with. Both Isaac and Mr. Evans were well satisfied with the established Church of England as it was. Isaac was steady and conventional. When his education had been completed, he had come home to learn his father's business with confidence that he would one day take full responsibility for the management of the estates. He was not a wild young man, but he enjoyed hunting and other pleasures which his sister considered "worldly." One of these was his annual birthday celebration, which must have been dulled by his sister who very grudgingly supervised the preparation of the feast. Isaac had no interest in his sister's gloomy religion of self-denial. Mary Ann, on the other hand, insisted on trying to convert him to her views.

Mary Ann's interest in religion was not unique; all of England was in a state of religious ferment. The Church of England had been napping through the early part of the previous century. Leaders among the clergy were from the upper classes. First-born sons inherited their father's estates; second-born sons were educated for the Church. With proper political and family connections a young man could expect to take over a parish and a sizable income, which would be his for life. These clergymen were complacent. They lived comfortably, enjoyed some prestige in their neighborhoods, and performed what few duties the Church required of them.

They were not prepared for John Wesley, a young clergyman who methodically sought to live according to the teachings of the Bible and the Prayer Book. At the age of thirty-five he "felt my heart strangely warmed." He spent the next fifty-two years riding on horseback throughout the British Isles preaching the saving grace of Jesus to growing crowds of enthusiastic listeners. Although Wesley always supported the Church, his followers broke away after his death. Mary Ann's uncle and aunt, Mr. and Mrs. Samuel Evans, were Methodists. At a time when few women spoke publicly on any subject the aunt went about the countryside preaching in fields and homes, visiting prisons and seeking converts. Other sects were also growing. The Franklin sisters were Baptists.

In response to this enthusiasm for things spiritual, the Evangelical movement grew within the Church of England. Evangelicals like Miss Lewis were singleminded in their disdain for all things worldly and their devotion to the Bible and good works. There were also those within the clergy who reacted to the Evangelical movement by re-examining the English Church's ties to Rome. They rewrote the liturgy, began wearing elaborate vestments, and added candles and decorations to the churches. Generally speaking, the Evangelicals became "Low Church" and those who looked back to Catholicism became "High Church."

Although these various groups of Christians differed in what they considered to be important matters, they all believed in the divinity of Jesus; in the miracles of His birth, life, and death; and in the Bible as the "Word of God." Another very small group were Unitarians. They doubted the miracles but accepted the moral teachings of Jesus. In addition there were Catholics, Jews, and a growing number of atheists in England.

Every age has its dominant call to action. During the past decade, many Americans have devoted time, print, talk—a great part of their lives—to the protection of the environment. To an even greater extent, nineteenth-century Englishmen devoted themselves to religion and philosophy. Mary Ann Evans was, therefore, a child of her age. She read religious books. She discussed religion with those who agreed with her and those who did not. She also enjoyed making a show of her good works and pious thoughts.

Maggie Tulliver went through a similar religious experience and ". . . often lost the spirit of humility by being excessive in the out-

ward act; she often strove after too high a flight, and came down with
her poor little half-fledged wings dabbled in the mud."

Mary Ann's letters to Miss Lewis were filled with lofty thoughts
clothed in long, involved sentences. The following comes from a letter
written when Mary Ann was eighteen:

> For my part, when I hear of the marrying and giving in marriage
> that is constantly being transacted, I can only sigh for those who are
> multiplying earthly ties which, though powerful enough to detach
> their hearts and thoughts from heaven, are so brittle as to be liable
> to be snapped asunder at every breeze. . . . I must believe that those
> are happiest who are not fermenting themselves by engaging in proj-
> ects for earthly bliss, who are considering this life merely a pilgrimage,
> a scene calling for diligence and watchfulness, not for repose and
> amusement.

This letter and others like it are reminiscent of the child who wanted
people to think her a very clever little girl. At least she was aware of
her vanity. "Instead of putting my light under a bushel, I am in danger
of ostentatiously displaying a false one," she wrote to her Methodist
aunt. "I feel that my besetting sin is . . . ambition, a desire insatiable
for the esteem of my fellow creatures."

In the summer of 1838 Isaac took Mary Ann to London for a short
vacation. Assuming that he was trying to please her, the trip must have
been a disaster. She refused to go to the theater with him and insisted
on staying in her hotel room reading spiritual books while he went
alone. She was "not at all delighted" with London, she wrote to Miss
Lewis, but what she liked best was the Greenwich Hospital. They went
to St. Paul's, where her strongest feeling was "indignation" toward the
people who performed the chanting—"a mere performance."

Having refused to enjoy the pleasures of London, she then decided
to give up musical performances. She had gone to hear an oratorio in
Coventry with that good Baptist lady Miss Rebecca Franklin. Later she
wrote to Patty Jackson that she was not planning to waste her time and
money on so sinful an activity again. "I think I can not justify the using

of an intensely interesting and solemn passage of Scripture as a rope-dancer uses her rope."

By the following spring she had found yet another worldly pleasure to denounce—novels. The only fiction she could approve were standard works like *Don Quixote, Robinson Crusoe,* the works of Shakespeare, and a few others. She recalled that as a little child "I could not be satisfied with the things around me; I was constantly living in a world of my own creation, and was quite contented to have no companions, that I might be left to my own musings, and imagine scenes in which I was the chief actress." No more such frivolity! "The weapons of the Christian warfare were never sharpened at the forge of romance." Presumably Miss Lewis chuckled over this letter while she was reading the famous George Eliot novels.

While she was busy denouncing most of the pleasures of the world, Mary Ann continued to study, though it is difficult to see how German and Italian would help save her soul. She also wrote a perfectly dreadful poem which was published in 1840 in the *Christian Observer.* The first of the ten verses, each of which ended with "farewell," follows:

> As o'er the fields by evening's light I stray
> I hear a still, small whisper—"come away;"
> Thou must to this bright, lovely world soon say
> Farewell!

She was planning to compile a monumental chart which would outline church history from the Roman Empire up to the Reformation. Like many would-be authors, she did more talking than actual writing. Mrs. Newdigate, the mistress of the Arbury estate, was interested in the project and urged her to use the extensive library at the manor house. She had also planned how to spend the profits from the publication of her chart. Some of the money would go to the local church. The rest was for "a favorite project of my own."

A few weeks later she wrote that she would not be preparing the chart after all; it had been just published by someone else. "I console all my little regrets by thinking that what is thus evidenced to be a desideratum has been executed much better than if left to my slow fingers and slower head."

If Mary Ann's piety were to be recorded on a graph, the line would start when she was nine years old and first met Miss Lewis. It would climb steadily until the time of her mother's death, when it would leap upward and continue to rise throughout her teen-age years. The line would then begin to waver downward and then plunge drastically.

The wavering had already begun when she bought herself a complete set of Wordsworth's poems for her twentieth birthday. She apologized for her self-indulgence, but the poems delighted her. She went on to read Byron, Shelley, and other Romantic poets. The interest in Romantic poets may have had something to do with her own emotions. Soon after her birthday she wrote her Methodist uncle that she could not give a hopeful account of her spiritual state because she had been "exposed to temptation from contact with worldly persons." One of these worldly persons may have been the "beloved object" she referred to in a letter to Miss Lewis the following month. Although the letter was so veiled in obscure phrases as to be unintelligible, it does seem that she had a brief romance. She suggested that hers were the first prayers to be offered up specially on his behalf, from which we may infer that he was a "sinner." She also went to a dance that winter, but the feeling that she was not in a "situation to maintain the Protestant character" combined with the "oppressive noise" produced a headache and then hysteria "so that I regularly disgraced myself."

During this year, 1840, Isaac became engaged to Sarah Rawlins, a woman ten years older than he. While visiting in Sarah's home, Mary Ann went to hear *The Messiah* one day and "some beautiful selections from other oratorios" the next. It had been just two years since she had declared oratorios to be repugnant to her.

In this same year Patty Jackson introduced her to the "language of flowers." Patty signed herself "Ivy," which meant "constancy." She gave Mary Ann the name "Clematis," which meant "mental beauty." Delighted, Mary Ann sent away for the flower book and gave Miss Lewis the name "Veronica," "fidelity in friendship." It is difficult to imagine the Mary Ann of a year or two earlier wasting her time on anything so frivolous.

It was not only Mary Ann's mental attitudes that were changing in 1840. With Isaac's engagement, changes had to be made at Griff. Much as she had hated her housekeeping chores, Mary Ann had to have mixed feelings about another woman taking over her responsibilities. She was probably relieved, therefore, when Mr. Evans decided to retire, leaving his duties and his house to Isaac. He and Mary Ann leased a house in Coventry, which they moved into in 1841.

∽ 5 ∾

THE DISTANCE from Griff to the new house in Coventry was only five miles. Nevertheless the move represented an enormous change in Mary Ann's life.

The house itself was attractive and well situated on the outskirts of the town. It was attached to another house in which lived Mr. and Mrs. Abijah Pears. Mrs. Pears was deeply involved in the Evangelical movement, and within a short time she had become a good friend to both Mary Ann and her father. The Franklin sisters welcomed their former pupil back to Coventry and were anxious to introduce her to their friends. She could not have been lonely.

Furthermore, her family should have given her deep satisfaction. Mary Ann was a bridesmaid at her brother's wedding in June, and she seems to have truly loved her new sister-in-law. She delighted in her role as aunt to Chrissey's two little boys. In July they came to visit her. That same year Chrissey gave birth to her first daughter, Mary Louisa, named after her aunt. Her half-sister Fanny, whom she had hardly known in her childhood, had married and lived just a few miles from Coventry. Fanny and Mary Ann became very close. Her father was making an adjustment to retired life.

Family and friends were not enough. She missed Griff. More importantly, she lacked the essential all-in-all person. Isaac had not been that person since she went away to school. Marriage had now irretrievably separated them. Her father had been her all-in-all, but only for short periods during her childhood. In her late teen years she had thrown her passion into her love of God. That faith was now breaking down. She had begun to observe that goodness and Christianity were not necessarily one and the same. Her beloved Scott portrayed heroes who were morally upright without the benefit of the Christian faith. All around her were professed Christians whose behavior was far from righteous.

> I have of late felt a depression that has disordered the vision of my mind's eye and made me alive to what is certainly a fact . . . that I am *alone* in the world [she wrote to Miss Lewis that summer]. I do not mean to be so sinful as to say that I have not friends . . . but I mean that I have no one who enters into my pleasures or my griefs, no one with whom I can pour out my soul, no one with the same yearnings, the same temptations, the same delights as myself.

Miss Lewis may have sensed a change in her beloved pupil. Certainly their relationship was changing. For years she had addressed her teacher respectfully as Miss Lewis. Mary Ann had then given her the playful flower name. Finally she had asked if she could drop the artificial name in favor of Maria, Miss Lewis' given name.

Maria Lewis was herself in a period of crisis. After serving as governess in the same home for many years, she was looking for a new position. Mary Ann was not only sympathetic, she was actively trying to help. She wrote about a job she had heard of from Fanny. A week later she wrote that there were boys at the school mentioned so they could dismiss that idea and wait for something more propitious. Apparently Miss Lewis would only teach girls. She discussed Miss Lewis' problem with her tutor, the same man who had been coming to Griff and then continued the lessons in Coventry. Another possible position was rejected because the family seeking a governess was not sufficiently pious. Miss Rebecca Franklin was ill, and a teacher was needed to take her place at the Franklin School. Miss Lewis, however, was too staunch a supporter of the Church of England to accept or be accepted by the

Baptist sisters. Finally in January, after a short visit in Coventry, Miss Lewis went to a new position in a school in Nuneaton. Hopefully, it was an all-girls school nestled under the right religious umbrella. Miss Lewis needed all the comfort she could find in her new surroundings to cope with the shattering change in her favorite pupil.

The instrument of change was the pious Coventry neighbor Mrs. Pears. She arranged for her brother and his wife, Charles and Cara Bray, to meet Mary Ann. Mr. Bray was an atheist. Mrs. Bray was a Unitarian. Mrs. Pears hoped that their heretical thinking would be influenced by the Evangelical faith of the intellectual Mary Ann. How wrong she was! The Brays were indeed impressed with the young lady—and she with them. At their first meeting they discussed a book written by Mrs. Bray's brother Charles Hennell, *An Inquiry Concerning the Origin of Christianity.* That book dealt the death blow to Mary Ann's already wavering faith.

In his book, published in 1838, Charles Hennell rejected the miracles and saw Jesus as a political leader as well as a moral and religious teacher. He believed that Jesus was a product of his time. Born when the Jews were chafing under the domination of Rome, Jesus combined religious fervor and a spirit of moral reform with patriotic zeal and a powerful personality. Many Jews welcomed him as the awaited Messiah who could deliver the Hebrew nation from the Romans. He was arrested and executed by other Jews who saw him as a pretender and who were anxious to preserve public peace lest Rome step in to deprive them of their last remnant of independence. These views of Charles Hennell were soon adopted by Mary Ann.

Within a few days Mary Ann was writing to Miss Lewis:

> My whole soul has been engrossed in the most interesting of all inquiries for the last few days, and to what result my thoughts may lead, I know not—possibly to one that will startle you; but my only desire is to know the truth, my only fear to cling to error. I venture to say our love will not decompose under the influence of separation, unless you excommunicate me for differing from you in opinion.

Even with that warning, Miss Lewis must have been shocked when she discovered that her pupil had swept from wholehearted piety to wholehearted rejection. Miss Lewis was visiting when Mary Ann first refused to attend church with her father. Two weeks later when Miss Lewis went on to her new school, Mary Ann was still avoiding church.

The father-daughter war was on! Robert Evans was an old man who had supported the Church of England all his life. He was a prominent member of the local congregation and enjoyed being called upon to pass the collection plate. "Nice" people all supported the Church of England. Some of them, it is true, made him a bit uncomfortable with their zeal for the Evangelical movement. Mary Ann had been too pious, but he had been confident that her views would become more moderate as she grew older. Never had he considered that she could swing to the opposite extreme. The Brays, in spite of their relationship to Mrs. Pears, were obviously not nice. Decent people did not question the authority of the Gospels. It was his duty to force his daughter's mind into his own mold.

Robert Evans amassed his troops—friends and family. Mrs. Pears, no doubt feeling guilty for her part in introducing Mary Ann to the Brays, presented all of the arguments of Evangelicalism. Miss Rebecca Franklin, who had helped to form Mary Ann's mind in the past, now tried to reform it. Unsuccessful in her attempts, she called in a Baptist minister. He, too, was unsuccessful. Miss Rebecca had introduced Mary Ann to the family of the Reverend John Sibree. He joined the fight and called in a professor of theology to assist him. Finally Robert Evans arranged for Fanny and Isaac to meet them at Chrissey's home. Isaac pleaded with his little sister.

Mr. Evans had one more weapon in his stockade—the threat of leaving her homeless to provide for herself. He would give up the house in Coventry and move into a small cottage he owned. He would not invite Mary Ann to go with him.

Mary Ann was just as rigid as her father. She was interested in truth, she said. Much as she hated the idea of teaching and the scanty meals and grim lodgings that went with a teacher's salary, she was willing to make any sacrifice for the cause of truth. The battle also appealed to her sense of drama. There was no doubt now that she was a very important person, one whose mind her friends and family were willing to fight for. She might even have enjoyed the Holy War except that she could not face separation from her father. She tried to discuss her faith—or lack of it—with her father. He would not listen. Finally she wrote him a long, pompous letter in which she said that she could not "without vile hypocrisy" join in worship of which she did not approve. "This and *this alone* I will not do even for your sake—anything else however painful I would cheerfully brave to give you a moment's joy."

Robert Evans was unmoved. Less than a week later Mary Ann was complaining to Mrs. Bray that no one in her family even cared what became of her. She was wrong. Isaac wrote to invite her to come to stay with him until conditions in Coventry would have cooled down a bit. She went to Griff on March 23.

For a time Mary Ann enjoyed being back at Griff. Isaac and his wife Sarah were kind to her. She took lovely long walks in the familiar countryside. But Griff was only a stopping place. She needed a home.

Sarah, apparently a pacifist until this time, entered the battle on Mary Ann's side. The two had become even closer during this visit, and Sarah finally convinced her father-in-law to allow Mary Ann to come home. She told him that his actions were precisely those which would make his daughter the most stubborn. If he were to invite her to return to the comforts of his home, she might quietly and gradually return to conventional religious thinking.

Mr. Evans abandoned his plans to move. Mary Ann went home on May 1. Soon after her return, Mr. and Mrs. Samuel Evans came for a short, painful visit. The two old Methodists had loved this niece who had put an insurmountable barrier between herself and them.

Mary Ann surrendered on May 15 when she went to Trinity Church with her father, but it was only a token surrender. She continued to think her own thoughts.

Late in the month Mary Ann wrote to Miss Lewis to invite her to spend part of her vacation in Coventry. She also told her teacher about the death of Chrissey's third child and Mary Ann's namesake. Her "little life of smiles and roses that seemed the promise of a healthy maturity" ended at the age of fifteen months. The letter was signed "your truly affectionate Mary Ann," but it is the last surviving letter from the girl to her former teacher. Miss Lewis came to visit Mary Ann a few more times, but they had grown too far apart. Thirty-two years later, hearing that her old teacher was retired and suffering financial hardships, Mary Ann wrote to her enclosing a gift of ten pounds. (The gift was repeated every year.) Miss Lewis wrote back saying that she had followed her pupil's career as George Eliot with interest. "My heart has ever yearned after you."

BOOK II

Marian

✑ 6 ✑

BACK IN COVENTRY, Mary Ann spent many hours each week at Rose-hill, the Brays' lovely home on the outskirts of Coventry. There her personality began to blossom, stimulated by amusing friends who were her intellectual equals.

Charles Bray, a man in his early thirties, had so many enthusiasms they fairly tripped over one another. He had inherited his father's prosperous ribbon manufacturing business, which provided him with a substantial income while requiring only a small portion of his energy. Much of his time was devoted to ideas, people, and causes.

Like Mary Ann, he had been committed to Evangelical Christianity in his youth. Then, while trying to convert a Unitarian minister, he began to question his own faith. He eventually renounced all religion. He had come to believe that the mind and personality are predetermined and cannot be changed. He had written two books espousing this philosophy: *Education of the Feelings* and *The Philosophy of Necessity*.

His views were supported by the new "science" of phrenology, which he adopted. According to phrenologists, the mind is revealed in the shape of the head. The brain is divided into areas controlling intellect, emotions, etc. By carefully measuring the head and observing all of the bumps and bulges, the phrenologist claimed to be able to read a personality. Charles Bray, of course, insisted that Mary Ann have a cast made of her head so that he could study it. Her unusually large head was a grand specimen. The cast showed that she had a large intellect. In the area of feelings, the animal and moral regions were about equal, but Charles Bray predicted that the moral would dominate the animal. Her cast also showed that her social feelings were active and that she was very affectionate, always requiring a man to lean upon.

Charles Bray believed that though people could not be changed, society could be made to serve human needs. He therefore threw himself into social reforms of all kinds—education of the poor, humane treatment of the insane, trade unions, socialism, freedom of speech and religion, extending the vote, etc., etc. His enthusiasms were too numerous to have been deep, but he was generous, gregarious, and jolly.

His wife, Caroline (always called Cara) Hennell, was only five years older than Mary Ann. The youngest of eight children, she had been raised a Unitarian, a faith she clung to with deep reverence. She seems to have been a nearly ideal woman, with her fine mind, musical and artistic talent, sweet disposition, femininity, and loyalty. Cara had been a governess before her marriage, and in Coventry she organized a school for the young children of the poor. Mary Ann helped her with her school. The two became dear and lifelong friends. Cara painted Mary Ann's portrait in watercolors during 1842. Even seen through the eyes of a loving friend, the girl is homely but with a sweet, wistful expression. Her dark hair is gathered over her ears in masses of curls. Her face and nose are long, her mouth wide, her eyes small.

Soon after Mary Ann's return to her father's house in 1842, Sara Hennell, Cara's older sister, came to Rosehill for a long visit. Brilliant and pedantic, Sara, too, became a lifelong friend. They wrote hundreds of letters to one another and obviously enjoyed long theological discussions. Sara's interest in theology—she wrote a number of books—never wavered. Mary Ann's did. Their common bond was thus weakened, but their affection remained.

Rosehill rang with music and talk. Cara and Mary Ann played piano duets. Groups of musicians often gathered and everybody played and sang. Interesting—often eccentric—people were invited to Rosehill. *What* guests thought was not nearly as important as *that* they thought. Robert Owen, a socialist advocate of communal living groups in America and England, was a guest. Another was Dr. Ullathorne, the son of a grocer who went to sea at age fifteen, was converted to Catholicism at age eighteen, and joined the Benedictine order. Eventually he was sent to Australia and later to Coventry where he wrote *The Catholic Mission in Australia.* Mary Ann, who had never been out of England, described him to Sara as one "who has shivered among ice-bergs, been broiled between the tropics and seen the wonders and beauties of the old world and the new."

Several years later Ralph Waldo Emerson, the essayist and philosopher from Massachusetts who was on a lecture tour of England, came to Rosehill. The Brays, Mary Ann, and Emerson went to Stratford on Avon, returning to Rosehill for tea. By the time Emerson left, less than twenty-four hours after his arrival, he had formed a favorable impression of Mary Ann Evans. "That woman has a calm, serious soul," he told Charles Bray. As for Mary Ann, she wrote Sara that Emerson was "the first *man* I have ever seen."

There could have been no objection to Emerson, but men like Owen and other lesser-known radicals were too much for Isaac. His goal for his sister was a suitable marriage—that is, a marriage to a man similar to himself, industrious and conservative. Isaac accused Charles Bray of being a rabble-rouser. His fear was that his sister should marry one of the other rabble-rousers she was apt to meet at Rosehill. He therefore urged his father to move Mary Ann away from the Bray influence. Mary Ann was confident that Isaac was motivated by brotherly devotion for her welfare—she always believed the best in Isaac. It is possible that she was right. It is also possible that Isaac was motivated by the selfish fear of having to provide for an old maid sister.

Fortunately for Mary Ann, her father refused to move. He was quite satisfied with his home in Coventry now that his daughter was attending church with him. Furthermore, Mr. Evans could not wholly disapprove of the Brays. His neighbor Mrs. Pears was one of his great favorites. Since she remained on friendly terms with the Brays, why shouldn't Mary Ann?

Mary Ann also traveled with the Brays and Sara. Most of these trips, each lasting a week or two, were within England. One was into Scotland. Not far, but adventures for Mary Ann.

Although she was happier than she had ever been before, there were still low and turbulent times. Mary Ann matured very slowly and was still behaving with the impetuosity of a teen-ager when she was well into her twenties. Just before her twenty-fourth birthday she went to London for the wedding of Elizabeth (always called Rufa) Brabant to Charles Hennell. After the wedding she went home with Dr. and Mrs. Brabant, the bride's parents.

Cara Bray saw Dr. Brabant for what he was, a silly old man with great pretensions of learning. He was forever talking about the book he was writing but never got beyond the introduction. Mary Ann worshiped him. Her letters to Cara were filled with rapture. "I am in a little heaven here, Dr. Brabant being its archangel. . . . Time would fail me to tell of all his charming qualities. We read, walk and talk together and I am never weary of his company. . . . Dr. Brabant spoils me for everyone else."

Mrs. Brabant, who was kind to Mary Ann at first, was blind. Her sister, who also lived with them, was soon suggesting the best train for Mary Ann to take back to Coventry. Within a few weeks Mrs. Brabant herself was demanding that Mary Ann leave. She did. As for the doctor, he denied ever having done or said anything to encourage the hero worship which his wife found so offensive. Years later, Mary Ann had her revenge. Dr. Brabant appeared as Mr. Casaubon in *Middlemarch,* one of George Eliot's most vivid and pitiful characters—the consummate humbug.

It was soon after this that Mary Ann had a brief romance. Known facts are few. She met the young man, a picture restorer, at the home of her half-sister, Fanny. Three days after meeting him, he proposed to her through Fanny's husband. She returned to Coventry and they exchanged letters. Cara said that Mary Ann was overflowing with happiness and that, though she did not love him yet, she admired his character so much that she thought she soon would love him. When he came to visit her in Coventry, she suddenly changed her mind and decided she could never love him enough to marry him. She sent him on his way, and then she was thoroughly miserable. Evidence again of the pressure on young ladies of that time to get married. Mary Ann may have felt that in refusing this young man she was accepting the unattractive life of the Victorian old maid.

ℰ 7 ℰ

SHE WAS stumbling along emotionally but she was striding intellectually. In 1844 she began her first major work, the English translation
of *Das Leben Jesu* by David Friedrich Strauss. Published in Germany a
few years before Hennell's *Inquiry* was published in England, Strauss'
book was a milestone in Biblical criticism. When Charles Hennell had
been asked to find a translator for the book, he had given it to his sister
Sara. She soon found her German to be inadequate. It was then given
to Rufa, who made a start but gave up the project soon after her
marriage to Hennell. Rufa suggested that the project be turned over
to Mary Ann.

In retrospect, Rufa was wise. It took Mary Ann two years of hard
labor to finish the fifteen hundred pages. In addition to the German
there were Latin, Greek, and Hebrew quotations to be translated. Mary
Ann sent each chapter of her translation to Sara for her criticism and
approval, and much of the correspondence between the two was devoted
to discussion of the precise English word to convey Strauss' meaning.
Within six months she was thoroughly sick of the project. Translating
can only be described as tedious. As time went by Mary Ann's sympathy
for Strauss' more extreme views certainly diminished. Mary Ann knew
and cherished the Bible to an extent that is incomprehensible to most
modern Americans. She had read it many times. Throughout her life

her letters and her books would be studded with quotations from both the Old and New Testaments. Although she no longer accepted the Bible as literal truth, she valued its moral concepts. Strauss' dissection of the Gospels was, therefore, frequently painful to her.

She knew, too, that her rewards were to be few. Her total pay for two years work was twenty pounds, about one hundred dollars. Her name would not even appear on her work. To put a woman's name on a scholarly work would be to damn it. "I do not think it was kind to Strauss to tell him that a young lady was translating his book," she wrote to Cara Bray. "I am sure he must have some twinges of alarm to think he was dependent on that most contemptible specimen of the human being for his English reputation."

She struggled on in spite of her weariness with the project. She also worried a great deal—first, that no one would read the book and second, that the publisher would not advertise it. At last it was finished. *The Life of Jesus, Critically Examined* was published by John Chapman in three volumes in June 1846. Then she worried about the reviews. Strauss himself wrote that he was delighted with the translation. A reviewer called her work "a faithful, elegant, and scholarlike translation."

Throughout the years that she was working on the Strauss—indeed throughout most of her life—she suffered from severe headaches. Events in her later life proved that she was given to "tension headaches." She also had dental problems. In 1848 she was given the newly introduced chloroform to have two teeth "dragged" out, and then she suffered a reaction to the chloroform which left her with another excruciating headache.

With Strauss behind her, she enjoyed a brief period of general light-heartedness. "If I am pious one day," she wrote to Sara, "you may be sure I was very wicked the day before and shall be so again next week." She wrote anonymous articles, several of them amusing, for the Coventry *Herald,* which Charles Bray had just purchased.

She also wrote a funny letter to Sara. In it she pretends that a German professor "whose musty person was encased in a still mustier coat" had come to England to secure a wife-translator. He is the author of twenty volumes, all of them unpublished, for which he blames the envy of rival authors. Although he has found many translators, none of them meet all of his qualifications—knowledge of English and German, ugliness, and a personal income. In his quest, the professor has been sent to Coventry. In Miss Evans he at last finds the perfect woman and proposes on the spot. She, thinking this may be her last chance at matrimony, accepts immediately. Her father objects because the professor is a foreigner, but nevertheless he, too, realizes that it may be her last chance and thus gives his consent. The wedding will take place next week and Sara is invited. Sara responded with a letter supposedly written by the professor in which he backs out of the engagement because Miss Evans is not, after all, ugly enough.

Mary Ann went to London where she heard Mendelssohn's *Elijah* conducted by the composer. She also read widely, sometimes frivolously. She spoke out in defense of the books by that immoral French lady, George Sand. She also read *Jane Eyre,* which she criticized. She was in favor of self-sacrifice but not for so ignoble a cause as the law which chained Mr. Rochester to his mad wife.

It was not long, however, before family problems began to intrude on her gaiety. Chrissey's life with Dr. Clarke had been marked by too little money and too many babies. Although Mr. Evans had tried on several occasions to rescue his son-in-law from financial disaster, Dr. Clarke was irretrievably bankrupt in 1848. That same year a nine-month-old boy died of whooping cough. There were still five little children to provide for and Chrissey would give birth the next year and again in 1851.

Then, too, Mr. Evans' health had begun to fail. By the spring of 1848 Mary Ann had made up a bed for him in the dining room so that he would not have to climb the stairs to his bedroom. She herself was sleeping on a couch to be near him. He had great difficulty breathing, which she blamed on the "imperfect action of the heart."

Through the years Mary Ann and her father had learned to live together peacefully, but they had each made independent lives for themselves. In his illness Mr. Evans became extremely demanding. In May she took him to the coast, hoping that his health and spirits would benefit from the change. He did improve briefly but returned to Coventry at the end of June as ill as when they had set out. In the meantime she was reading the Scott novels aloud to him. "Father . . . makes not the slightest attempt to amuse himself, so that I scarcely feel easy in following my own bent even for an hour," she wrote to the Brays. "I look amiable in spite of a strong tendency to look black, and speak gently though with a strong propensity to be snappish."

Cara, on the other hand, reported to Sara that while their friend was keeping up her spirits through her ordeal, she looked like a ghost. She also reported that Mr. Evans was finally beginning to show some gratitude to his daughter.

In September Isaac told his father that the doctor had said that death could come at any time. Mr. Evans made his will. If he felt any special warmth or gratitude for his youngest daughter, it was not revealed in that final document. He divided his property between his sons Robert and Isaac. Fanny and Chrissey had each been given one thousand pounds when they were married and were to receive another one thousand pounds each. Mary Ann was to receive two thousand pounds in trust, which meant that she was to receive only the interest on the money, and one hundred pounds in cash. To Fanny he gave silver forks and the set of Scott novels which Mary Ann had been reading aloud to her father all during his illness. Chrissey was to have her mother's Bible. He left Mary Ann no remembrance.

Still the old man lived on. Mary Ann wrote hurried notes to her brothers and sisters reporting on the state of their father's health. She humored his every wish. "My life is a perpetual nightmare and always haunted by something to be done, which I have never the time, or, rather, the energy, to do," she wrote to Sara in February of the next year. Although she was growing very tired, she seemed to be finding peace in knowing that she was doing everything that could be done for her father in his last days.

Robert Evans died on May 31, 1849.

❧ 8 ❧

LESS THAN two weeks after her father's death. Mary Ann was on her way to France with Charles and Cara Bray. The Brays had been planning the trip for some time. When Mr. Evans died, they convinced Mary Ann that she should accompany them. A change of scenery was just what she needed, they thought. They were wrong. Exhausted from her months of nursing and benumbed with a sense of loss, Mary Ann was miserable. She was both ill and irritable.

They left England on June 11, 1849, traveled through France into Northern Italy, and arrived in Switzerland the middle of July. There Mary Ann came to her senses enough to realize that what she needed was not activity but solitude, a chance to sit quietly, grieve, and then plan for her future. She decided to stay in Switzerland. Charles Bray helped her to find suitable lodgings, and then he and Cara continued their trip homeward through Germany.

Mary Ann lived for three months in a pension (a sort of hybrid between a small hotel and a boarding house) just outside of the city of Geneva. It was beautifully situated on the lake, surrounded by lovely old trees and with a view of the mountains. Here, at last, Mary Ann could reassemble the shattered pieces of her life.

She had always felt a desperate need to be needed. No one needed her now. She was almost thirty years old, well into spinsterhood. The one hundred pounds her father had left her would see her through the year, but the interest on the two-thousand-pound trust fund would never be adequate for her living expenses. Should she try to teach? She still abhorred the idea. Furthermore, with her liberal views, she would be rejected by most schools and families. Could she earn a living translating? Having labored two years on the Strauss for a miserable twenty pounds, that possibility seemed hopeless. Could she write original articles and reviews? She had probably received nothing for her articles for the Coventry *Herald* except the satisfaction of helping a friend.

Novels? Cara Bray had suspected that she was writing a novel during her Coventry days. Whether she actually made a start or merely discussed the idea, no one now knows. At the pension she did make a few notes for a novel. She *must* have enjoyed imagining herself as the Jane Austen of her century. She certainly did begin to develop her ability to write bright, amusing sketches of people and personalities. Following are bits and pieces of letters written to the Brays which demonstrate this talent while revealing something of her life at the pension:

> . . . I find no disagreeables, and have every physical comfort that I care about. The family seems well-ordered and happy. I have made another friend, too . . . a pretty old lady with plenty of shrewdness and knowledge of the world. She began to say very kind things to me in rather a waspish tone yesterday morning at breakfast. I liked her better at dinner and tea, and today we are quite confidential. I only hope she will stay; she is just the sort of person I shall like to have to speak to—not at all "congenial," but with a character of her own. The going down to tea bores me, and I shall get out of it as soon as I can. . . . The American lady embroiders slippers—the mamma looks on and does nothing. The marquis and his friends play at whist; the old ladies sew; the madame says things so true that they are insufferable. . . .

Life at the pension was pleasant; it was not perfect. Mary Ann never heard enough from her family in England, and the news she did hear was sometimes sad. Chrissey lost another child, Clara, who died of scarlet fever at the age of seven. "That angelic little being had great interest for me," Mary Ann wrote to Fanny. "She promised to pay so well for any care spent on her."

She was frequently worried about money and wrote to Charles Bray asking if it were possible to sell her Encyclopedia and globes for half of what she had paid for them.

Then there was the Sibree affair. Mr. Sibree was one of the Coventry ministers called in to try to save Mary Ann's soul during the Holy War. The Sibrees had two children, both a few years younger than Mary Ann. Mary Sibree had studied German with Mary Ann. John Sibree had been a ministerial student. She corresponded with both of them. When both of their children rejected the religion they had been taught at home, Mr. and Mrs. Sibree had been quick to blame Mary Ann. That autumn, old Mr. Sibree was in Europe and dropped in unannounced on Mary Ann at her pension. The visit was extremely unpleasant.

A few weeks later, Mary Sibree asked Mary Ann to write to her in care of the Brays rather than to her own home. That was the kind of hypocrisy that Mary Ann could not tolerate. She chose instead to discontinue the correspondence, asking the Brays to convey this decision to the girl. "She is a sweet good girl, but her ideas want testing. . . . Also, there is a strong leaven of Sebreeanism in her which . . . is that degree of egotism which we call bad taste but which does not reach to gross selfishness—the egotism that does not think of others, but would be very glad to do them good if they did think of them—the egotism that eats up all the bread and butter and is ready to die of confusion and distress after having done it."

The pension became less attractive as winter approached, and Mary Ann decided to move into the city of Geneva. Luckily she found a bedsitting room in the private apartment of M. and Mme. d'Albert Durade.

M. d'Albert was an artist who had studied for the ministry and had not even begun to draw until after he was twenty-one years old. As a result of a childhood accident, he was not more than four feet tall, with a deformed spine but a fine head. He was obviously brilliant, refined, and charming. During that winter he painted Mary Ann's portrait. Later he was to translate her novels into French. They corresponded throughout her life. He is generally believed to have been the model for Philip Wakem, a small, deformed young painter and musician, who adored Maggie in *The Mill on the Floss.*

Mme. d'Albert was described by Mary Ann as having less genius and more cleverness than her husband. Her household, her sons, and her servants were all well managed. The food was delicious, and Mary Ann told the Brays that she made "a spoiled child of me."

Although Mary Ann was their boarder, the d'Alberts made her feel like a guest whom they were delighted to honor. They invited her to meet their friends and to join musical evenings with them. She enjoyed their conversation. "I learn something every dinnertime," she wrote. "They are people worth sitting up an hour longer to talk to."

She spent the winter quietly, taking walks every day, playing the piano which she had rented for her room, reading Voltaire, and attending daily lectures on physics. Yet when spring came she was anxious to return home.

Unmarried ladies, even thirty-year-old ladies, seldom traveled alone in those days, and M. d'Albert accompanied her back to England. The railway was not open all of the way from Switzerland into France so they had to cross the mountains in sledges, huge horse-drawn sleighs. They arrived in London on May 23, 1850. The next day Mary Ann rushed off to her friends in Coventry.

She had been away for nine months. As she approached her home she began to imagine ever more joyful reunions with those whom she loved. She was disappointed. March in England is gray, damp, and cold. Coventry countryside is flat and dull. It was the town where she had spent the last years with her father, and her feeling of loss returned to her.

"We are apt to complain of the weight of duty, but when it is taken from us, and we are left at liberty to choose for ourselves, we find that the old life was the easier one," she wrote to Patty Jackson.

After a few days with the Brays she set off on a round of family visits. Isaac must have been more horrid than usual. In Switzerland she could remember the Isaac she had adored in her childhood. Back at Griff she wrote, "It was some envious demon that drove me across the [mountains] to come to see people who don't want me." She was already asking Sara to look around for a suitable boarding house in London for her.

By May she was visiting Chrissey. If the weather improved, her spirits did not. "I have been so ill at ease ever since I have been in England. . . . Dear Chrissey is much kinder than anyone else in the family and I am happiest with her. . . . But I am delighted to feel that I am of no importance to any of them, and have no motive of living amongst them," she wrote to Cara.

Within a few days, she was back in Rosehill with the Brays. There M. d'Albert visited her for three days before his return to Switzerland. Except for brief family visits and two weeks in London, she lived at Rosehill until the end of the year.

It was a year of change. The most obvious one was Mary Ann's name. She changed it to Marian while she was in Switzerland. The change could have caused little inconvenience to the Brays and Sara—as soon as she had ceased to be Miss Evans to them, she had become either Polly or Pollian. Other changes were more momentous. Charles Bray suffered serious business losses. Charles Hennell died of tuberculosis, leaving Rufa with a four-year-old son.

It was also the half-century mark in a rapidly changing England. During the first fifty years of the nineteenth century, the population of England had doubled and shifted. People who had depended on the farms for their livelihood at the beginning of the century were streaming into the textile and iron centers. Locomotives that had been non-existent were chugging across the countryside on five thousand miles of track, dividing farms and connecting towns and villages that had been isolated from one another just twenty years earlier. With the industrial revolution, England had become the richest and most powerful nation in the world.

The ideals of the bloody revolution in France had crossed the English Channel, and political power was gradually seeping away from the privileged few giant titled landholders (like the Newdigates of Arbury Hall). Democracy had spread to the ever-expanding middle-class factory owners and managers, professional men, small landholders, tradesmen, and artisans. But the upper and middle classes comprised no more than a third of the English population. The rest were the masses who tilled the land they did not own or slaved long hours in the mills and mines for a few pennies a day. They lived in poverty and ignorance, without representation in the "democratic" government.

Queen Victoria, who was exactly the same age as Marian Evans, had already ruled England for thirteen years, had been married for ten, and was the mother of five children. Of the two the complacent queen was certainly more "typical" of her age than the middle-class intellectual who was still struggling to find her place in English life.

❧ 9 ❧

IN OCTOBER John Chapman and Robert William Mackay came to Rosehill. Chapman was the publisher of Mackay's books *The Progress of the Intellect, as Exemplified in the Religious Development of the Greeks and Hebrews* as well as Marian's translation of *The Life of Jesus*. Since Mackay's views were similar to those of Strauss, Marian was asked to review the new book for the *Westminster Review*. In November she delivered her piece to Chapman in London and stayed in his home for two weeks, returning to spend a few more weeks with the Brays and Christmas with Chrissey.

On January 8, 1851, she was back in London to take up residence at 142 Strand, Chapman's home, office, and bookstore, which had been built originally as a hotel. The Chapmans still took in paying guests, many of whom were literary people like Emerson, William Cullen Bryant, and Horace Greeley from the United States.

John Chapman was twenty-nine years old, handsome and intelligent, with a well-established reputation as a lady's man. Mrs. Chapman, fourteen years older than her husband, had but one obvious asset —her small fortune. They had been married seven years and had three children, two of whom lived at home and one, a deaf-mute, who lived with an uncle. The children's governess, Elisabeth Tilley, was a pretty young woman who charmed and was charmed by her employer.

Marian found life at 142 Strand to be delightful at first. She lived much as she had lived the previous winter in Geneva—a rented piano in her room, classes in geometry at the Ladies College, a lecture by Faraday at the Royal Society. In addition, intelligent people with interesting ideas were frequent guests for an hour, a day, or longer.

One thing she needed desperately was a paying job. She edited a novel which Chapman planned to publish, but she was not paid. She and Chapman both tried to find commissions for her to write reviews of new books. All they received were rejection notes.

John Chapman took a great interest in her welfare and obviously delighted in her company. Mrs. Chapman and Miss Tilley did not. They both grew to resent the affection that Marian and Chapman showed one another. Before the end of March Marian was back with the Brays.

Two months later, Chapman came to Rosehill to solicit her help. When an eccentric English gentleman offered to back Chapman in publishing a liberal quarterly magazine, Chapman bought the *Westminster Review,* the transfer to become effective on October 8. Although Chapman himself lacked the necessary scholarly qualifications, he would be editor-in-chief of the magazine. What he needed was someone to do the actual work while he basked in the glory of the title. Marian was just such a person, and he came to Rosehill to discuss the new magazine with her. Marian, still needing to be needed, began work at once. An insurmountable barrier remained. If she were to edit the *Westminster Review* she would have to spend most of her time in London. Mrs. Chapman and Miss Tilley refused to accept her back at the Strand or in any other lodgings in London.

During the summer Marian came to London with the Brays to see the fabulous Crystal Palace which had just opened in Hyde Park. One of the monuments of the Victorian era, the Great Exhibition of industrial wonders and works of art was housed in a huge structure of glass and iron. While they were in London, Chapman brought his wife to call on Cara Bray. Marian was present. In September Chapman took his wife to Rosehill. Again Marian was present. Mrs. Chapman finally agreed to allow Marian to return to 142 Strand on September 29—

same room, same piano, but an entirely businesslike relationship with Chapman.

Beginning in January 1852, Marian edited ten issues of the *Review,* which came out four times a year. Each of the truly distinguished issues contained articles on reform, politics, history, religion, popular science, and reviews of books. She suggested articles and authors to write them, edited manuscripts, and wrote reviews. There is no indication that she was ever paid a penny for this work but she probably received free room and board. With the interest from her trust fund it was thus possible for her to exist, but in no very grand manner.

Enter Herbert Spencer. Destined to become one of the great philosophers of his century, Spencer's first book, *Social Statics,* had just been published by Chapman. More importantly, during the year 1852 he would write an essay, "The Development Hypothesis," in which he expressed the idea of evolution––seven years before Charles Darwin shocked the world with the same idea in his *Origin of Species* (Darwin did not steal from Spencer; they were just two of several who arrived at the same destination at roughly the same time by different routes). In the same year in an article entitled "Theory of Population," Spencer also coined the phrase "the survival of the fittest." Spencer was to devote his life to the idea of evolution, expanding it to include the development of the mind, social institutions, and morals.

Spencer was the same age as Marian. His education had been spotty but his experience varied. After working as a civil engineer, planning new lines and bridges for the ever-expanding railway, he had become a subeditor of *The Economist* with offices just opposite the Chapman establishment on the Strand. He was a frequent visitor to the Chapmans. Within a short time of Marian's return to London, Spencer became her daily companion, taking her to the opera and for long walks. Mutual friends began to anticipate their engagement. Spencer wrote enthusiastically about her mind to a friend. Her lack of beauty was one great barrier to love, or so Spencer led people to believe. They must have discussed marriage because Marian wrote the Brays that they had decided that they were not in love. But she did enjoy being with Spencer. He was a pleasant and intelligent companion who appeared in her life at a time when she had all but given up hope of marriage. One can imagine that she would have liked to have been in love with him, certainly that her friends encouraged it, but not that she ever cared very deeply.

During the summer she spent two months on the coast of Kent. Spencer visited her there. They were still seeing one another in the fall. By winter, however, he had received a small inheritance and was off on a tour of the Continent. Nothing Spencer saw in Europe pleased him. Although he was healthy enough to climb a number of peaks in the Alps, he returned a fussy hypochondriac with palpitations of the heart and other vague symptoms which he never tired of discussing. He was often seen taking his pulse in public. He protected himself from exciting conversations by wearing ear plugs. In spite of his "ill health," he was a prodigious worker and writer who lived to be eighty-three years old.

Spencer had few friends and yet he remained close to Marian for the rest of her life. Nevertheless, even after Marian was dead, he continued to deny that they had ever been engaged. He protested too much! Whatever he may have said, he kept a picture of the ugly woman whom he had never wanted to marry beside his bed until the day he died. He destroyed all of her letters except for six which he had sealed away, not to be opened until 1985. Will they reveal anything new about the Marian Evans-Herbert Spencer relationship? We will know in a few years.

Spencer was not the only interesting person in Marian's life during her years with the *Westminster Review*. She met a number of fascinating people, like Thomas Huxley, Charles Dickens, and Wilkie Collins. Two women of special importance because they became lifelong friends were Bessie Rayner Parkes (later Mme. Louis Belloc) and Barbara Leigh Smith (later Mme. Eugene Bodichon). Both were several years younger than Marian, the daughters of extraordinarily liberal fathers and destined to become active feminists.

Bessie was the author of a volume of poems which were published by Chapman in 1852. The Parkes family invited Marian to dinner parties which she obviously enjoyed. When they invited her to a ball, she declined the invitation because she had no appropriate gown. "At a dinner-party, when people think only of conversation, one doesn't mind being dowdy," she explained to Bessie, but she could not appear at a dance looking "like a withered cabbage in a flower garden." Bessie, who tended to be insensitive and single-minded, became co-editor of the *English Woman's Journal,* which was devoted to women's rights.

It was Bessie who introduced Marian to Barbara Leigh Smith, a warmhearted young lady who refused to be restricted by either corsets or conventions. Unlike her cousin Florence Nightingale, who was forced to fight her family for the right to practice nursing, Barbara had a father who had always given his children a great deal of freedom. (Her mother had died, leaving Barbara, age seven, and four younger children.) Wealthy Mr. Smith chose to educate his children at home, leaving them free to study whatever they chose. When Barbara demonstrated a talent for drawing, she was provided with the best teacher available. She became an accomplished landscape painter. Mr. Smith also had the peculiar idea that daughters should receive the same financial provisions as sons. He gave her an ample allowance when she came of age and later left her a small fortune, much of which went to help further feminist causes. She also furthered the cause by refusing to wear the uncomfortable clothes dictated by fashion and by traveling around the Continent unchaperoned.

In spite of interesting people, Marian was in deep despair when she returned to London in the fall of 1852. She was approaching her thirty-third birthday; she had been disappointed in her relationship with Herbert Spencer. Nothing was going right. "You may as well expect news from an old spider or bat as from me," she wrote to Cara. "Nothing happens to me but the ringing of the dinner-bell and the arrival of a proof." She continued to be despondent through much of the long winter. The *Review* never quite pleased her. She decided she was a miserable editor. She was frequently headachy.

Problems at home added to her misery. Chrissey's husband died in December, leaving his wife with six children ranging in age from fifteen months to fifteen years. Marian and Isaac both rushed to the aid of their sister. Dr. Clarke's life had been a financial disaster, and after paying off his debts Chrissey was left with less than enough to live on. Isaac offered her a small cottage on his property. Marian decided that the most helpful thing she could do was to hurry back to London to try to earn money to send to her sister. She made the decision without consulting Isaac, a serious error. Isaac was indignant and "flew into a violent passion." He ended his tirade by telling Marian that he wished her never to "apply to him for anything whatever." As Marian pointed out to her friends at Rosehill, this was a silly statement since she had never asked him for anything in the past. Still, Isaac would never be an out-and-out cad in his sister's book. She continued her letter, saying that Isaac "is better than he shewed himself to me and I have no doubt that he will be kind to Chrissey, though not in a very large way."

A few months later someone offered to send Chrissey's children to an orphanage. The suggestion was probably made in a kindly spirit—one can only hope that it did not come from Isaac—but Chrissey was devastated. Marian went to support her. Another suggestion was that Chrissey and the children should move to Australia. Marian considered going with them just to help them get settled, but Chrissey was no pioneer and chose living in near poverty in England to life in Australia.

✑ 10 ✑

THE WINTER of Marian's discontent was followed by a radiant spring. "People are very good to me," she wrote to Cara. "Mr. Lewes, especially, is kind and attentive, and has quite won my regard, after having had a good deal of my vituperation. Like a few other people in the world, he is much better than he seems. A man of heart and conscience, wearing a mask of flippancy."

Herbert Spencer had introduced Marian to George Henry Lewes (pronounced Lew-is) in October of 1851. Her first reaction to him was negative. He certainly was not physically attractive. He was small. Even people who liked him said that he looked like an ape. His cheekbones were broad, his jaw narrow, and his bushy eyebrows and moustache gave his pockmarked face an allover hairy look. His eyes were his redeeming feature. They were deep-set, dark, and expressive.

Some people—Marian may have been among them at first—said that his manner was brash. Others characterized him as amusing and charming. He loved jokes and told them well. His banter, which could be counted on to enliven any party, made him a sought-after guest.

He was certainly hard-working and intelligent. He wrote reviews and articles for almost every issue of the *Westminster Review* which Marian edited. In addition he wrote pages of reviews for the weekly *Leader,* which he and Thornton Leigh Hunt had founded in 1850. He also translated and adapted plays and wrote articles for other publications. Although he was just two years older than Marian, he had already published his four-volume *Biographical History of Philosophy,* two novels, and a biography. He was working on *Comte's Philosophy of the Sciences.* In the past he had lectured and taught. The grandson of a famous-in-his-day comedian, Lewes even appeared on stage occasionally. So much productivity may have seemed dubious to Marian. How could any man who did so much do anything well? The fact is that he delved deeply into subjects that interested him and wrote well. Marian soon grew to have deep respect for his work.

Marian met George Lewes as a friend of Herbert Spencer. Their work for the *Review* threw them together. Gradually he began to visit the Strand more and more often and to invite Marian to the theater more and more frequently. By the spring of 1853 he had no doubt told her of the personal misery which he kept carefully hidden behind his public gaiety.

At the age of twenty-three he had married a beautiful and intelligent nineteen-year-old, Agnes Jervis, with whom he had four sons. The youngest boy died of whooping cough and measles before his second birthday. Two weeks later, Agnes gave birth to a fifth boy who had been fathered by Thornton Leigh Hunt, Lewes' business partner and friend. The Hunts and the Leweses were all unusually liberal-minded and had given lip service to the idea of free love. Lewes, therefore, claimed the baby as his own and had him registered as Edmund Alfred Lewes. He forgave Agnes, and he and Hunt continued to work together on *The Leader.* Until Agnes became pregnant with a second Hunt child. (Agnes eventually gave birth to four Hunt children while Hunt continued to live with his own wife by whom he had nine children.) As far as Lewes was concerned, his marriage to Agnes was over before he had met Marian. Free love, which had seemed an acceptable theory, had proved to be an absolutely repugnant fact.

Unfortunately, he could not obtain a divorce. Divorce in Victorian England was exceedingly rare—no more than one for every thousand marriages. A man could only obtain a divorce on grounds of adultery.

By condoning Agnes' first offense he had forfeited his right to legal action when she repeated it. (The divorce laws were even more difficult for women. A woman could not obtain a divorce on the grounds of adultery alone but had also to prove cruelty, desertion, or a criminal act. Even then her divorce required an Act of Parliament.)

Lewes' sons—who were five, seven, and nine when their father moved out of their home—continued to live with their mother, but Lewes visited them often and supported them, their mother, and the other children. He was, therefore, under tremendous financial pressure. He was also emotionally distraught and physically ill. Here, at last, was a man who needed Marian Evans.

The winter of 1853 was hectic for Marian, too. She was not happy living with the Chapmans and thought and talked of moving. John Chapman begged her to stay. His finances were in a disastrous state; they would be worse if he had to pay her to edit the *Review.* The magazine had been well received among intellectuals and praised for its quality, but it was still losing money.

In June Chapman advertised the publication of an English translation of Ludwig Feuerbach's *Das Wesen des Christentums.* Marian was to do the translation for two shillings a page—about thirty pounds. As she worked, she again sent her translations to Sara Hennell, who checked them carefully against the original.

In the fall Marian finally moved out of the Chapman household into two tiny rooms on Cambridge Street. She continued to edit the *Review* and to work on her translation. When Chapman decided not to publish the Feuerbach after all, Marian was indignant. At last, she showed signs of standing up and fighting for her own welfare. "I bitterly regret that I allowed myself to be associated with your Series, but since I have done so, I am very anxious to fulfill my engagements both to you and the public," she wrote to Chapman. "I don't think you are sufficiently alive to the ignominy of advertising things, especially as part of a subscription series, which never appear. . . . Consider the question of Feuerbach as one which concerns our *honour* first and our pockets after."

She won the battle. Feuerbach's *The Essence of Christianity* was published in June 1854 with Marian Evans' name on the title page. It was the only time that her real name ever appeared on a published book.

What Feuerbach had to say was of exceptional interest to his translator as she coped with her growing love for Lewes. The German philosopher believed that the highest good is that which man creates himself and which gives him pleasure. Marriages of convenience, entered into without love, he held to be immoral, while marriages based on love and entered into spontaneously were the truly moral unions.

She also fought with Chapman on Lewes' behalf. Two books on Comte's philosophy were published at about the same time. One was by Lewes, the other by Harriet Martineau. Chapman sent both books to Thomas Huxley for review. Huxley praised the Martineau book to the skies and tore Lewes' book to shreds. Marian begged Chapman not to publish the review at all. This time the silent editor of the *Westminster Review* lost to the titular editor.

Lewes, who was a frequent visitor in Marian's new home, was sick during the winter and spring of 1854. While she continued to edit the *Review* and to work on her translation, she wrote many of his columns for *The Leader.*

Marian was also unwell. In all likelihood her ill health reflected the turmoil in her mind. George Henry Lewes was everything she longed for in a husband. She tended to be overly solemn; he was witty and gay. She tended to be pessimistic; he was optimistic. He was kind, generous, and intelligent. He was a good companion and friend. And she loved him. For years she had sought some one person who would be all-in-all to her and to whom she would be all-in-all.

But they could not marry as long as Agnes lived. Although Marian had renounced formal Christianity, she believed with all her heart in the Christian ethic, in striving for moral goodness, in living for others. She also believed in truth and honesty. She could not live the life of a secret mistress. But could she live openly with George Lewes without marriage? She discussed her dilemma with Charles Bray and John Chapman. Both men advised against it. She would cut herself off from all respectable society, they warned her. Intellectual and liberal men in Victorian England could expect their friends to either ignore or be amused by infidelity; women could expect nothing but social abandonment.

She could not consult Isaac. They had grown far apart over the years. Had they remained close, it is doubtful that she could have taken a step which she knew to be in direct opposition to all that he believed in. Chrissey was the only member of the family who cared what she did, and Chrissey was too involved in her own problems to notice what was going on in London.

Lewes was determined to provide for Agnes and his sons whatever his future life might bring. Marian, with her strong conscience and her desire to do right, was just as determined as he that no one should suffer for any action she might take.

In June, Marian went to Rosehill for the last time. She did not have the courage to tell Sara and Cara what she was planning to do. On July 10 she returned some books and a painting to Sara, explaining that she was preparing to go abroad.

On July 19 she wrote this letter: "Dear friends—all three—I have only time to say good-bye, and God bless you. *Poste Restante,* Weimar, for the next six weeks, and afterwards Berlin. Ever your loving and grateful Marian."

Back and forth she paced on the deck of the *Ravensbourne.* Her head throbbed; her hands felt clammy. *Where is he? Could he have been detained? No, of course not. He is coming. He must come. It is my fault. Why did I arrive early?*

Marian's eyes were floating in tears. She tried to breathe deeply. It was impossible. People were milling around her, bumping into her. Porters. Ship's officials. Passengers. Well-wishers. The only sensible thing to do was to go to her cabin and sit quietly. She could not sit quietly. *He will come.*

But where is he now? Panic. She must not panic. She watched the people boarding, her eyes darting from face to face. He had to be among them. And then she saw a hand raised in greeting, and his beloved twinkling eyes appeared above a porter's shoulder.

They ran toward one another. She longed to throw herself in his arms but she was a mature woman of thirty-four. They smiled at one another as she slipped her arm through his.

The passage to Belgium was glorious. "The sunset was lovely, but still lovelier the dawn," she confided to her journal. "The crescent moon, the stars, the first faint blush of the dawn reflected in the glassy river, the dark mass of clouds on the horizon, which sent forth flashes of lightning, and the graceful forms of the boats and sailing vessels, painted in jet-black in the reddish gold of the sky and water, made up an unforgettable picture. Then the sun rose and lighted up the sleepy shores of Belgium, with their fringe of long grass, their rows of poplars, their church spires and farm buildings."

All night long Marian Evans had strolled the deck of the *Ravens-bourne* with the man she loved. Till death, he would be her all-in-all.

BOOK III

Mrs. Lewes

❧ 11 ❧

ANY HOPE the elopers might have had of slipping away silently was shattered when they met Robert Noel on the deck of the *Ravensbourne*. The Noel family and the Bray-Hennell families were close friends. Robert Noel would have been a rare man had he not mentioned the encounter when he wrote to England.

After a few days in Antwerp and Brussels, Marian and George boarded a train for Cologne. Again fate presented them with a man from their past—Dr. Brabant, the dishonorable "archangel" of Marian's youthful "heaven." The old man offered to introduce her to David Friedrich Strauss, the author of *The Life of Christ,* who was staying in Cologne. On July 30 Dr. Brabant brought the author to meet his English translator. The meeting was "rather melancholy," Marian confessed later to Charles Bray. "Strauss looks so strange and castdown, and my deficient German prevented us from learning more of each other than our exterior which in the case of both would have been better left to imagination."

The trip to Germany was not intended as a vacation—such a luxury was beyond their means—and so they hurried on to Weimar, which was to be their home for three months. George was gathering material for what was to become one of his greatest books, his biography of Goethe. Johann Wolfgang von Goethe (1749–1832) was a poet, dramatist, scientist, and statesman whose *Faust* is considered to be one of the masterpieces of world literature. He had spent much of his life in Weimar.

Although Marian was a nobody, George was a recognized scholar who had lived in Germany before. He had many friends and contacts anxious to entertain him and his wife.

On August 10 Franz Liszt called on the Leweses and invited them to breakfast in his garden. A number of other writers and artists were present. Marian was captivated by her host. "Genius, benevolence, and tenderness beam from his whole countenance, and his manners are in perfect harmony with it," she gushed. With the first drop of rain, the party moved indoors, and to Marian's delight Liszt sat down at the piano to play one of his own compositions. "I sat near him, so that I could see both his hands and face. For the first time in my life I beheld real inspiration—for the first time I heard the true tones of the piano. . . . His manipulation of the instrument was quiet and easy, and his face was simply grand—the lips compressed, and the head thrown a little backward."

It was a happy time filled with work. Marian wrote an article for Chapman. She was also translating Spinoza's *Ethics.* They attended the opera and the theater. Almost every day they took a long walk in or near the delightful town. Evenings, when they did not go out, they read aloud to one another. Their greatest joy, however, was simply in being together. She wrote Charles Bray that their first month together had been one of "exquisite enjoyment." On August 30 she wrote John Chapman, "I am happier every day and find my domesticity more and more delightful and beneficial to me. Affection, respect and intellectual sympathy deepen."

Fortunately, they were not aware of the boiling gossip vat in England. Uninformed acquaintances were passing along stories about how George Lewes had deserted his innocent wife and children to run off with a godless woman. Their bliss was shattered in October when they received a letter from Thomas Carlyle, warning them of the rumors. Carlyle, one of Scotland's most famous men of letters—essayist, biographer, and historian—was a friend for whom George had the greatest respect. He could be sure that the older man's motives were pure and that conditions were just as he reported them. Marian and George spent an almost sleepless night reading and rereading the letter. Marian wept. In the morning George wrote to Carlyle and to Arthur Helps, another essayist and historian, who was also a great friend. The letters have been lost, but a week later George wrote again to Carlyle to thank him for his sympathy: "I have honoured and loved you . . . both as teacher and friend, and *now* to find that you judge me rightly, and are not estranged by what has estranged so many from me, gives me strength to bear what yet must be borne."

Marian wrote letters of explanation to John Chapman and Charles Bray. She asked Charles Bray to contradict the report that Lewes had run away from his wife and family. He and his wife were in frequent correspondence, she received all the money due him in England, and his children were his chief concern. ". . . His conduct as a husband has been not only irreproachable, but generous and self-sacrificing to a degree far beyond any standard fixed by the world. . . ." She was worried about how Sara and Cara would receive this gossip. "I am quite prepared to accept the consequences of a step which I have deliberately taken and to accept them without irritation of bitterness. The most painful consequences will, I know, be the loss of friends. If I do not write, therefore, understand that it is because I desire not to obtrude myself."

Sara answered that letter with what must have been a critical and accusing letter, for Marian's response was full of explanations and ended with a pathetic plea: "I love Cara and you with unchanged and unchangeable affection, and while I retain your friendship I retain the best that life has given me next to that which is the deepest and gravest joy in all human experience."

In November Marian and George left Weimar for four happy months in Berlin. The city was dull and unattractive. The weather from January on was bitterly cold, but Marian recalled how they battled their way home from dinner against winds and snow to enjoy long evenings in their warm room reading and sipping hot coffee and munching on cookies and rolls. They also continued to work. George interviewed people who had known Goethe and heard this story: After meeting a man he did not like Goethe said, "I thank thee, almighty God, that thou hast produced no second edition of this man." As in Weimar, they enjoyed the opera, the theater, and friends.

Back in England in March, they separated for the first time in eight months. Marian took lodgings in Dover while Lewes went to London. His purpose was business. He had first to see his sons and pay his wife's bills. He had also to find a publisher for his Goethe biography and sell some of his articles. He had a desperate need for money! He may also have been "testing the wind" in London to see how Marian would be received. He was a man of the world and knew that she would be much more severely criticized than he for the elopement. After spending about three weeks in London he went on to visit his friend Arthur Helps.

Meanwhile, Marian was living in limbo. She worked on her Spinoza translation and took long walks along the cliffs of Dover. She read extensively, and she wrote long letters telling Sara and Bessie Parkes how calm and happy she was. Yet she was frequently sick. Although George wrote to her regularly, she must have suffered agonizing moments of doubt. If Agnes and the boys begged him to return, would duty prove stronger than love? Was he strong enough to withstand the blasts of scandal?

What must have been one of very few happy moments during her five weeks of solitude came in the form of a letter from John Chapman. He asked her to write the book review columns for the *Westminster Review*. This would not only be pleasant work for her, it would also bring a regular income.

The ordeal of solitude ended on April 18 when Marian met George in London. They spent two weeks in temporary lodgings, five months in East Sheen, and then moved to lodgings in Richmond, which they were to occupy for three years.

During their first two weeks in London, they had three visitors—John Chapman, Rufa Hennell, and Bessie Parkes. For the two women, the calls represented acts of courage. Rufa was motivated by affection for Marian. Bessie, too, was sincerely fond of Marian, but she was also a feminist whose attitudes were colored by what she thought was good for the movement. She saw Marian's defiance of convention as delicious freedom—akin to Barbara's refusal to wear corsets. Bessie never seemed to understand that Marian's elopement was based entirely on personal need and had nothing whatsoever to do with women's rights. Tactless Bessie insisted on addressing her as Miss Evans, and Marian wrote several times to remind her that she was not known by that name. They were Mr. and Mrs. Lewes to each of their landladies, good Christians who would never knowingly harbor an unmarried couple.

Not that Marian was left unmoved by feminist causes. At that time married women had no control over their own finances. Everything a woman either earned or inherited was the property of her husband. It was possible for a man to squander even a very large fortune left to his wife by her family. Barbara Leigh Smith drew up a petition asking Parliament to pass a law granting married women a legal right to their own money and property. Marian not only signed it but also sent a copy to Sara, asking her to gather signatures in Coventry.

John Chapman continued to need Marian's help and was a frequent visitor. In June he brought her an article he had written himself, "The Position of Women in Barbarism and Among the Ancients." He wanted her criticism and he got it. After reading the article carefully, she wrote that she liked it but, " '. . . Suffice it to say' is the peculiar property of hack writers. Don't infringe on their domain. . . . 'On the one hand' and 'on the other hand' are rather too frequent. . . . Your sentences would often be very much improved by being broken up. . . ." Chapman obviously took her criticism with bad grace because she was writing two days later to say that of course his article was worth publishing. "I think it is very valuable and interesting; indeed I thought I had said so in my letter. It is for that very reason that I dwelt on certain defects of style which you can remedy by giving a little more trouble. The opening of the article would be really beautiful if the sentences were pruned a little." Chapman was obviously satisfied; the article appeared in the October *Review.*

The trio at Rosehill were the friends she would most like to have seen. Time and again she wrote to Charles Bray asking him to come. Twice she sent detailed instructions for getting to their lodgings in East Sheen. He did come on July 10, but the visit was a disappointment to Marian. Both she and George had colds, and George and Charles argued about phrenology.

For some time Charles' ribbon business had been failing. At the age of forty-five he was forced to retire. He devoted the remaining twenty-eight years of his life to his enthusiasms—reforming and writing—but he was never again to enjoy financial prosperity. He sold Rosehill to John Cash, the husband of Mary Sibree, and he and Cara moved to nearby Ivy Cottage.

Sara continued to write but the old intimacy was gone. Marian's gifts of autographs for Sara's collection almost seem to be bribes to keep Sara writing. Finally in October, Sara did muster her courage to make an unannounced call. Unfortunately, Marian and Lewes were out when she arrived.

Sara had been Marian's friend of the intellect but it was Cara to whom Marian had turned for warmth and personal understanding. Cara did not write for almost a year. When she did write it was apparently to ask Marian what she wanted done with some linens Marian had left at Rosehill. In the same letter Cara must have accused her of taking the institution of marriage lightly. In a very long letter, Marian told Cara to give those "dreadful sheets and pillow cases" away if she could not use them herself. She also tried again to explain her relationship to George.

> Assuredly if there is any one subject on which I feel no levity it is that of marriage and the relation of the sexes—if there is any one action or relation of my life which is and always has been profoundly *serious,* it is my relation to Mr. Lewes. . . . One thing I can tell you in a few words. Light and easily broken ties are what I neither desire

theoretically nor could live for practically. Women who are satisfied with such ties do not act as I have done—they obtain what they desire and are still invited to dinner.

Marian and George Lewes were definitely not invited to dinner. In fact, Marian seldom went anywhere except for long walks. George went into London once a week to see his sons and to conduct his business. During their first summer together in London, George took his sons to the coast of England for a brief vacation.

In spite of, perhaps even because of, what must have been a very lonely life, Marian was working more productively than she had ever worked before. So, too, was George. Years later she reported that they had but one small sitting room in Richmond and had to sit so close together when they were writing that the scratching of his pen nearly drove her wild.

George sold his *Life and Works of Goethe* to David Nutt, who published it on October 30, 1855. He received two hundred and fifty pounds on publication day and another one hundred pounds the following April. The book was well reviewed. Writing to Charles Bray, Marian said, "I can't tell you how I value it, as the product of a mind which I have every day more reason to admire and love." Less partial judges were also enthusiastic. Even today it is mentioned as one of the fine biographies of the German poet.

No publisher could be found for Marian's translation of Spinoza's *Ethics,* but both she and George wrote many articles during the years 1855 and 1856. In addition to her regular columns for the *Westminster Review,* Marian wrote a series of recollections of Weimar for *Fraser's Magazine* and a number of other short pieces. A single issue of *The Leader* contained four articles by George and two by Marian.

George, who had frequently written on scientific subjects, decided to become a knowledgeable zoologist in 1856. He no doubt discussed his plans with Herbert Spencer, who returned from his long trip abroad and had dinner with his old friends on April 15. On May 8 Marian and George went westward to the sea to spend six weeks in Ilfracombe in Devonshire and six weeks in Tenby, on the southern coast of Wales.

She wrote extensive Ilfracombe recollections which can be summarized in a few sentences which she wrote to the Brays:

> We are enchanted with Ilfracombe. I really think it is the loveliest seaplace I ever saw, from the combination of fine rocky coast with exquisite inland scenery. But it would not do for any one who can't climb rocks and mount perpetual hills. For the peculiarity of this country is that it is all hill and no valley; you have no sooner got to the foot of one hill than you begin to mount another. . . . You would laugh to see our room decked with yellow pie-dishes, a *foot-pan,* glass jars and phials, all full of zoophytes or mollusks or annelids —and still more to see the eager interest with which we rush to our "preserves" in the morning to see if there has been any mortality among them in the night. . . . After this we mean to migrate to Tenby, for the sake of making acquaintance with its mollusks and medusae.

It was a happy summer, and in August the first of George Lewes' many *Seaside Studies* appeared in *Blackwood's Magazine.*

～ 12 ～

TENBY, on the south coast of Wales, was the birthplace of George Eliot the novelist. Except for one brief interlude in her priggish adolescence, Marian had been an avid novel reader all of her life. True, the novels were usually indulged in as a dessert following a heavy meal of classics, philosophy, and science, but she greatly admired the art of Sir Walter Scott, Jane Austen, Charlotte Brontë, George Sand, and William Makepeace Thackeray. Although she had dreamed of writing a novel herself, she had produced nothing more than one descriptive introductory chapter. George had read that chapter when they were in Germany. He knew that she could handle descriptions beautifully. The articles she had written during the first two years of their marriage had impressed him with the scope of her talent. He had eloped with a bright self-effacing and sympathetic woman. He was beginning to suspect her of genius. His one doubt was dramatic flare. Could she plot a story and write believable dialogue? He was anxious to find out. At Tenby, he urged her to try.

She began by thinking of novels in a general way and suggested to John Chapman that she write an article for the *Westminster Review* to be entitled "Silly Novels by Lady Novelists." Then one morning as she lay dozing in her bed she imagined herself writing a story entitled "The Sad Fortunes of the Reverend Amos Barton." The title delighted her. She woke George to try it out on him.

"Oh, what a capital title," were his first encouraging words.

Marian was ready to begin as soon as they returned to Richmond in August. She was no longer interested in the article on silly novels, but John Chapman liked the idea too much to release her. She decided to spin it off in a hurry to get on with her own fiction. She wrote it while George took a quick trip to Switzerland to place his two older boys in the Hofwyl School there.

Marian began *Amos Barton* on September 22. Soon after, she suggested to George that it might be the beginning of a series of stories to be entitled *Scenes of Clerical Life*. He expressed his approval, but his doubts about her ability to write fiction did not begin to disperse until she read the first part of her manuscript to him. A scene in a farmhouse where local people are gathered to drink tea and discuss the local curate, Amos Barton, convinced him that she had at least some of the qualities that had worried him. The hostess is an old lady who sits quietly in an easy chair "under the sense of compound interest perpetually accumulating which has long seemed an ample function to her." The local doctor is happily present, as he "is never so comfortable as when he is relaxing his professional legs in one of those excellent farmhouses where the mice are sleek and the mistress sickly."

The curate is a balding man of no particular distinction. "His very faults were middling—he was not *very* ungrammatical. It was not in his nature to be superlative in anything; unless, indeed, he was superlatively middling, the quintessential extract of mediocrity."

His wife Milly is a "gentle Madonna." The Bartons have six children and money is always scarce, but Milly somehow provides by darning the darns and patching the patches.

The flawed plot involves the parishioners' disdain for their pastor. Their disdain grows when an elegant countess moves into the vicarage for a few days and stays six months, demanding constant attention from the already overworked and unwell Milly.

On the night when Marian planned to write the climax of her story —Milly's death in childbirth—George went into London so that Marian could work undisturbed. She read the scene to him when he returned, and they cried over it together.

"I think your pathos is better than your fun," George said as he kissed her.

The Sad Fortunes of the Reverend Amos Barton was finished on November 5.

George Lewes was absolutely essential to the development of Marian Evans as a novelist. He kept her writing with his constant encouragement. He also managed all of her business affairs. One of his wisest business decisions was his selection of her publisher, the firm of William Blackwood and Sons. The distinguished Edinburgh publishing house had been founded in 1804. John Blackwood, the sixth son of the founder, had been born in Scotland and educated there and in France and Italy. He was then trained as a bookseller and given charge of Blackwood's London office. In 1852 he had taken command of the company, with responsibility for *Blackwood's Magazine* as well as for most of the books published by the firm. John Blackwood was a man of charm, tact, good judgment, and a talent for coddling temperamental authors. Lewes had contributed articles to *Blackwood's Magazine* for years, and his *Seaside Studies* were currently appearing there. Lewes also had contacts with many other publishing firms. His decision to offer *Amos Barton* to Blackwood was probably based on the fine reputation of the firm and the personality of its director.

On November 6, 1856, George Lewes wrote John Blackwood that he was sending a manuscript written by "a friend who desired my good offices with you. This is what I am commissioned to say to you about the proposed series," Lewes continued. "It will consist of tales and sketches illustrative of the actual life of our country clergy about a quarter of a century ago; but solely in it *human* and *not at all* in its *theological* aspect; the object being to [represent] the clergy like any other class with the humours, sorrows, and troubles of other men. He begged me particularly to add that—as the specimen sent will sufficiently prove—the tone throughout will be sympathetic and not at all antagonistic."

John Blackwood's reserved acceptance of *Amos Barton* was something of a disappointment to Marian. After a few hints from Lewes, Blackwood's negative comments were always well clothed in affirmative ones. When the first installment of *Amos Barton* appeared in the January 1857 issue of *Blackwood's Magazine,* she received a check for fifty pounds and a letter which would satisfy even the most praise-starved writer. Blackwood referred to the story as fresh, humorous, and touching, and wrote that "the style is capital, conveying so much in so few words."

In those days, magazine articles and stories were seldom signed. One of the pleasures of literary people was guessing who wrote particular pieces. The editor, of course, usually knew. John Blackwood was different. He had no idea who George Lewes' young friend was. Had he lived in London, he might have guessed, but he was in Scotland and probably knew little about Lewes' private life. He was an avid golfer; now he had a new sport—trying to identify his new author. Lewes delighted in egging him on. Bits of their correspondence read like "twenty questions."

Obviously the author is a clergyman.

No, he is not a clergyman.

A man of science?

No.

Blackwood's letters to his new author came in envelopes addressed to Lewes. The salutation was "My Dear Sir" and then "My Dear Amos." Finally, recognizing Blackwood's awkward position, Marian wrote that whatever might be the success of her stories, she was determined not to reveal herself. She would, however, offer a *nom de plume* "as a tub to throw to the whale in case of curious inquiries." That letter is signed George Eliot. She chose "George" because it was Lewes' name and "Eliot" for no other reason than that she liked the sound of it. Blackwood then looked up correspondence from a man who had a brother named Eliot, but the handwriting did not match.

The new name was useful to Marian as well as Blackwood.

"If George Eliot turns out a dull dog and an ineffective writer—a mere flash in the pan—I, for one, am determined to cut him on the first intimation of that disagreeable fact," she wrote.

On Christmas day she began *Mr. Gilfil's Love-Story.* A much longer story, she was still working on it when she and George set out in the spring for another seaside expedition. Before they left, George carefully planted the idea with Blackwood that he was going alone and would be handling his friend's manuscript by mail.

Actually, they left Richmond together, traveling by train and coach to Penzance, a coastal town on the extreme southwestern tip of England. Their destination was the Scilly Isles, little dots of granite in the Atlantic Ocean. They waited eight days in Penzance for one of the twice-weekly sailing days to coincide with decent weather. Once on the islands they were delighted and were soon off with their chisels and baskets in search of specimens for George's studies.

Mr. Gilfil's Love-Story, which was already appearing in installments in *Blackwood's Magazine,* was finished between long walks along the shore. This second Scene of Clerical Life opens and closes with the lonely, respected vicar, Mr. Gilfil. Few but the oldest of his parishioners remember him as a young man or can recall the bride he brought with him to Shepperton.

Unfortunately, the love story is a trite Victorian romance. The heroine, Caterina, is an Italian orphan who has grown up in the household of Sir Christopher Cheverel. Both Sir Christopher and his wife have made a pet of the child, loving her as they would have loved an adorable puppy or kitten. She has but one outstanding talent, a beautiful singing voice which gives both of her patrons great pleasure.

Two young men also spend much of their time at Cheverel Manor. One is Maynard Gilfil, a clergyman who has been Sir Christopher's ward. He has adored Caterina since childhood. The other young man is Sir Christopher's nephew and heir to the estate, Anthony. Caterina adores Anthony. A weak young man, he has enjoyed a flirtation with Caterina but intends to marry an aristocratic young woman whom he brings to the manor.

Driven to madness by her jealousy of Anthony's fiancee, Caterina goes out to meet him in the garden with a dagger in her pocket. When she finds him already dead—from a heart attack—she is filled with remorse and guilt and runs away. Maynard Gilfil finds her and eventually helps her to return to sanity. She marries him but dies in childbirth.

This is the love story of the dear old vicar who had "poured out the finest, freshest forces of [his] life-current in a first and only love."

From the Scilly Isles, George and Marian went on to the island of Jersey, a part of England located just off the coast of Normandy in the English Channel. In contrast to the bare rocks of Scilly, Jersey was lush with orchards and wild flowers. The seaside studies continued, and Marian wrote Sara that George "is this moment in all the bliss of having discovered a parasitic worm in a cuttlefish."

Meanwhile, speculation was growing as to the author of the *Scenes* which were appearing in *Blackwood's Magazine.* There were plenty of clues. The Newdigate family recognized the manorhouse described in detail in *Mr. Gilfil's Love-Story* as a direct copy of their Arbury Hall. They would have had to assume that the author was therefore someone who had visited their home. Isaac may not have read *Blackwood's Magazine,* but he would surely have heard conversations about the amazing similarity between the fictional and the real manorhouses. The church at Shepperton was also a copy of the church near Griff.

Marian kept up her correspondence with Sara, writing in loving detail about Sara's work, a book entitled *Christianity and Infidelity.* She also told Sara that she was not doing any more reviewing. Did Sara suppose that her industrious friend was devoting *all* of her time to cuttlefish?

She had stopped writing for the *Westminster Review* in January. Although John Chapman did his best to lure her back with offers of more money, she stubbornly refused to write anything for him. What did he think she was doing?

Marian's family was in her thoughts although she had not seen any of them for a long time. Chrissey and the two little girls who were still living at home had fallen prey to a typhus epidemic during the winter. One of the children had died. Chrissey was terribly ill. Marian had written Isaac from the Scilly Isles to ask him to give Chrissey fifteen pounds from her trust fund. She hoped that Chrissey would be able to use the money to get away for a little while as soon as she was able to travel.

In addition to worrying about Chrissey's health, she was also worrying that her family would hear of her relationship with George Lewes. Such rumors were already circulating in Coventry, according to Sara. What had arrived in Coventry would soon reach Griff. She would naturally want her family to hear the news from her rather than from a malicious gossiper.

While she was in Jersey—three years after her elopement with George—Marian wrote two letters, one to Isaac and one to Fanny, telling them that she was married. In both letters she wrote that she had married a man older than she—he was two years older—that they had three boys to support, that they were not wealthy but that they were both workers and that they could provide for themselves. She asked Isaac to deposit her yearly income, less the fifteen pounds for Chrissey, in Mr. Lewes' bank account in London.

Isaac was furious. He had once been angry because his sister did not consult him before scheduling a trip to London. How much worse that she should choose a husband without his approval. He was so grieved that he was unable to write himself and asked his lawyer to write for him to inquire when and where she was married (he must have heard some of the rumors), what her husband did for a living, and where he lived.

Whatever weeping Marian may have done when she received the letter from the lawyer, her response was a model of friendly restraint. She said she was glad that her brother did not write "if his feelings towards me are unfriendly." She went on to explain that "Mr. Lewes is a well-known writer, author among other things of the 'Life of Goethe' and the Biographical History of Philosophy. Our marriage is not a legal one, though it is regarded by us both as a sacred bond."

Fanny's response was more generous, and Marian wrote, "Thanks— a thousand thanks, dear Fanny, for your letter." Fanny must have also chatted about a Mr. Liggins, who was supposed to be the author of *Scenes*. "You are wrong about Mr. Liggins or rather your informants are wrong," Marian wrote. "We too have been struck with the 'Clerical Sketches,' and I have recognized some figures and traditions connected with our old neighborhood. But Blackwood informs Mr. Lewes that the author is a Mr. Eliot, a clergyman, I presume." Did Fanny really buy the

Liggins rumor—which was to grow and spread—or did she suspect her half-sister of the authorship and use the rumor to try to extract the truth?

Fanny wrote only one letter after the announcement of Marian's marriage. That letter had been written almost immediately, before Isaac had made his wishes known to his sisters. He himself would never write to Marian as long as Lewes lived. He wished Chrissey and Fanny to do likewise. Both women submitted.

Marian wrote one other letter to Coventry on the subject of her relationship with George Lewes. It was to Mary Sibree Cash, who was living in Rosehill with her husband and children. Marian had once been very close to the younger woman and she wished her to know the truth rather than the version told by the scandalmongers.

> I am very happy—happy in the highest blessings life can give us, the perfect sympathy of a nature that stimulates my own to healthful activity [she wrote]. I feel, too, that all the terrible pain I have gone through in past years partly from the defects of my own nature, partly from outward things, has probably been a preparation for some special work that I may do before I die. This is a blessed hope—to be rejoiced in with trembling. But even if that hope should be unfulfilled, I am contented to have lived and suffered for the sake of what has already been.

Marian and George returned to Richmond at the end of July. George made a hurried trip to Switzerland in August to see his sons. In September they received their first social invitation as a couple. In their three years together, Marian had never been invited to another woman's home. The first welcome invitation was issued by Rufa, the widow of Charles Hennell who had been one of Marian's first callers when she had returned from Germany in 1855. The invitation came soon after Rufa had married Wathen Mark Wilks Call, a former clergyman who had recently renounced his vows.

Just as Rufa was behaving with characteristic generosity, Bessie Parkes—the other early caller after the trip to Germany—continued to behave with characteristic tactlessness. In her feminist zeal she continued to address Marian as Miss Evans.

"It is Mr. Lewes' wish that the few friends who care about me should recognize me as Mrs. Lewes, and my Father's Trustee sends me receipts to sign as Marian Lewes, so that my adoption of the name has been made a matter of business," she wrote to Bessie.

The work at hand was the completion of the third Clerical Scene, *Janet's Repentance,* which she had begun in the Scilly Isles and continued in Jersey. Genial John Blackwood had had some qualms about Marian's first two stories. He had difficulty adjusting to the non-hero Amos Barton. Mr. Gilfil was a more satisfactory hero, but Caterina's intention to stab her lover hardly seemed suitable for a heroine. He suggested that Caterina should merely dream of killing her lover. Marian ignored his suggestion. In the published scene, Caterina steals the dagger and goes to the garden planning to use it.

The mediocre and the murderer were followed by the alcoholic. That the alcoholic should be a female and the heroine of the third Scene was almost more than the publisher could bear. All along he had been pleading for lightness, but the third story was even grimmer than its predecessors. It is to Blackwood's everlasting credit that he recognized his unknown author as a genius and quickly retreated from his suggestions rather than risk losing so great a talent.

Janet's Repentance is about a town and a couple divided. The townspeople are divided into factions, one supporting the old established church with its aging comfortable curate, Mr. Crewe, and the other supporting the devout young minister of the Evangelical church, Mr. Tryan. The Crewe supporters are led by a local lawyer and politician, Mr. Dempster. Dempster is unscrupulous and becomes increasingly brutal as he drinks more and more heavily. Much of his brutality is directed against his wife, Janet, a childless young matron who turns to wine for solace. Their relationship deteriorates to the point where Dempster throws his wife out into the street in her nightgown. In the depth of her degradation, Janet turns to the saintly Mr. Tryan for support in overcoming her drinking habit. It is a sordid tale—Dempster's delirium tremens and his final death following an accident caused by drunkenness are vividly recorded—with a bittersweet conclusion.

In spite of John Blackwood's misgivings, all three of the Clerical

Scenes appeared in *Blackwood's Magazine* and were published in a two-volume book in January 1858. George Eliot asked her publisher to send the new book to eight people whose opinions she sought. One of these was Charles Dickens, England's most popular writer. His letter is quoted below in its entirety, an example of a great man's generosity and insight.

My Dear Sir,—I have been so strongly affected by the two first tales in the book you have had the kindness to send me, through Messrs. Blackwood, that I hope you will excuse my writing to you to express my admiration of their extraordinary merit. The exquisite truth and delicacy, both of the humor and the pathos of these stories, I have never seen the like of; and they have impressed me in a manner that I should find it very difficult to describe to you, if I had the impertinence to try.

In addressing these few words of thankfulness to the creator of the Sad Fortunes of the Rev. Amos Barton, and the sad love-story of Mr. Gilfil, I am (I presume) bound to adopt the name that it pleases that excellent writer to assume. I can suggest no better one: but I should have been strongly disposed, if I had been left to my own devices, to address the said writer as a woman. I have observed what seemed to me such womanly touches in those moving fictions, that the assurance of the title-page is insufficient to satisfy me even now. If they originated with no woman, I believe that no man ever before had the art of making himself mentally so like a woman since the world began.

You will not suppose that I have any vulgar wish to fathom your secret. I mention the point as one of great interest to me—not of mere curiosity. If it should ever suit your convenience and inclination to show me the face of the man, or woman, who has written so charmingly, it will be a very memorable occasion to me. If otherwise, I shall always hold that impalpable personage in loving attachment and respect, and shall yield myself up to all future utterances from the same source, with a perfect confidence in their making me wiser and better. —Your obliged and faithful servant and admirer,

Charles Dickens.

Dickens also wrote to John Blackwood. Praising *Janet's Repentance,* he insisted that it could only have been written by a woman. "If I be wrong in this, then I protest that a woman's mind has got into some man's body by a mistake that ought immediately to be corrected."

Thackeray, who also received a free copy, spoke enthusiastically of *Scenes*. He was not as prescient as Dickens, however, and insisted that George Eliot was a man.

One of the most satisfying letters the new author received was from Mrs. Carlyle, the wife of George's old friend and teacher. She wrote that while she could not imagine why she had received the book, since she knew no one named George Eliot, she was most profoundly grateful. She had read the book one night when she had been too sick with fever and sore throat to sleep. It helped her through the dreary night better than "the most sympathetic helpful friend" could have done. She praised *Scenes* as the kind of book "that grows rarer every year—a *human* book—written out of the heart of a live man, not merely out of the brain of an author—full of tenderness and pathos, without a scrap of sentimentality, of sense without dogmatism, of earnestness without twaddle—a book that makes one *feel friends* at once and for always with the man or woman who wrote it!"

Although the published reviews were also favorable, the book sold only moderately well. The new author was the discovery of the literary few, not the novel-reading masses.

Major William Blackwood, a former army officer in India, was his brother's right-hand man in the publishing firm. John Blackwood seldom made an important decision without consulting him. In December Major Blackwood called on George Lewes in Richmond. Although all three parties apparently remained silent on the subject of George Eliot's identity, Marian wrote in her journal that she and George knew within a few minutes of the Major's arrival that he had recognized her as the mystery author. In February John Blackwood called, and when he asked if he might meet George Eliot, Marian left the room. Lewes followed her, and she told him that she might reveal her identity to her publisher. The Blackwoods were just as anxious as the Leweses to preserve the secret.

∽ 13 ∾

Scenes of Clerical Life was followed by George Eliot's first three full-length novels, published at yearly intervals. They were *Adam Bede* in 1859, *The Mill on the Floss* in 1860, and *Silas Marner* in 1861.

Adam Bede had been conceived as another in the series of *Scenes,* but as the story developed in Marian's mind, the clergyman retreated into the background and the narrative became too involved for anything short of a full-length novel. Blackwood's lack of sympathy for *Scenes* also helped her to decide that it was time to draw them to a close. In one of her early letters to her publisher she announced that the new work would be a "country story—full of the breath of cows and the scent of hay."

The plot is uncomplicated, with the action leading toward the trial and conviction of a teen-age mother accused of killing her own baby. The naive country girl, Hetty, has been seduced by the young squire who always meant to do the right thing but fell short of his goal. Adam Bede, a young carpenter, had wanted to marry Hetty, and he stands by her during her trial. After her conviction Hetty's cousin, a female Methodist preacher—also young—comes to the prison to stay and pray with her, and finally to accompany her to the gallows.

The novel is set at the turn of the nineteenth century. Adam Bede, whose weakness as a fictional character is his inhuman perfection, was modeled after Marian's father. Even Isaac was aware of the likeness and told a neighbor that there were incidents in the book that only his sister would know. Marian's peppery Methodist aunt bore no resemblance to the young preacher in the novel, but it was she who had told Marian about a prison visit to a young woman convicted of infanticide. The girl refused to confess her crime until Marian's aunt had spent a night in prison praying with her. Then at last the girl burst into tears and confessed. The aunt rode in the cart with her to the place of execution.

Marian gave the first part of *Adam Bede* to Blackwood in March. He was delighted with the new story—the clean country setting and the kindhearted characters—but he wanted to know more about how it would progress before he started it in *Blackwood's Magazine.* Marian refused to tell him. He had been dismayed by the dark realism in her *Scenes.* She could hardly expect him to be enthusiastic about a novel that included a seduction scene, an unwed mother, infanticide, and a less-than-noble squire. She and George decided that it would be better to skip magazine publication for this novel and present it for the first time in book form.

In April the Leweses went to Germany. They lived in Munich for three months, where their social life continually interrupted her work. Munich was followed by Dresden, where they knew no one. There they rented a large apartment, and Marian's delight in a room all to herself with a door she could close is pathetic. Here, at last, she could work without the distraction of George's scratchy pen. During the two months they were in Dresden, she wrote a major portion of the book. It was finished back in Richmond on November 16.

"I love it very much," she wrote in her journal about *Adam Bede,* "and am deeply thankful to have written it, whatever the public may say. . . ."

What the public said was "Bravo!" Within weeks of its publication, Blackwood wrote to Marian to say that "we may now consider the Bedesman fairly round the corner and coming in a winner at a slapping pace." A week later he wrote to say that he could now congratulate her on being a *"popular* as well as a great author." He was already planning a second edition, to be followed by new editions issued with gratifying regularity.

With the ever-increasing fame of *Adam Bede* came the ever-more-insistent question, "Who is George Eliot?" John Chapman thought he knew the answer. He asked Herbert Spencer point blank if Marian were the novelist. He hinted publicly that he knew the author personally and that the author was a woman. Marian was angry. She wrote asking Chapman how he would like to have a friend circulate unfounded reports, especially if he had shown by his every word and deed that he wanted the reports kept quiet. But John Chapman was slightly insensitive. He may also have been miffed because his former editor refused to write for the *Westminster Review* and jealous of another publisher's great success with her work.

London gossip was also fed by the obvious prosperity which the Leweses were enjoying. Soon after the publication of *Adam Bede* they had left their cramped lodgings and moved into a house in the country, Holly Lodge, complete with a servant and their own furniture. George Lewes' *Goethe* and *Seaside Studies* had been successful but not *that* successful. Acquaintances noticed the change in their living style and decided that *Adam Bede* might indeed have been their benefactor.

The gossip in London was as nothing compared to the stories circulating around Coventry. Fanny had written that Joseph Liggins was thought to be the author of *Scenes of Clerical Life.* The story of his authorship grew and spread. Charles Newdigate met John Blackwood in London and congratulated him on the series of stories he was running about Newdigate's country home and neighborhood. He told Blackwood that he knew the author, Mr. Liggins. Sara wrote asking Marian if she had read the two books by George Eliot and announced that they were written by Mr. Liggins, whom Marian might not have heard of since he was the son of a baker and of no importance in the area. Sara went on to relate this episode: A group of dissenting clergymen went to visit Mr. Liggins to ask him to write for their paper. They found him washing his slop basin at the pump. "He has no servant and does everything for himself, but [one of the parsons] said that he inspired them with a reverence that would have made any impertinent question impossible." Sara then commented on how strange it was that the *Westminster Review* should hint that George Eliot was a woman when everyone in Coventry knew that he was Mr. Liggins. "They say he gets no profit out of 'Adam Bede,' and gives it freely to Blackwood which is a shame."

Both Marian and George were briefly amused by the Liggins story—Marian wrote Blackwood that the real George Eliot had no intention of giving away his manuscripts no matter how much reverence that action might inspire. George asked Blackwood how he could bear to drink his wine from the skull of the poor man in Coventry.

Their amusement was short-lived. A letter appeared in the *Times* announcing Mr. Liggins as the author of the George Eliot books. The real George Eliot answered with a letter to the *Times* saying that Mr. Liggins was not the author. Then a group of men who believed that the villainous Blackwood had cheated poor Mr. Liggins began to solicit contributions for the needy author.

What was Marian to do? She could hardly allow Blackwood's reputation to be smeared—he had in fact been more than generous with her. Nor could she sit back and allow an imposter to collect charity. She suggested that if Liggins were really the author he should write a chapter to prove it.

The Brays and Sara, the three people to whom Marian had once felt the closest bonds, never even suspected Marian of writing the two books. Their blindness is almost inconceivable. They knew her style of writing, that she had wanted to write a novel, and that after years of regular writing for magazines she was no longer producing non-fiction. They also knew that she was as familiar with the area around Coventry as Liggins.

Only one old friend recognized Marian as George Eliot, and she did not even have the benefit of the complete books but had only read a few excerpts and reviews. She was Barbara Leigh Smith. In Algiers with her family, Barbara had met Dr. Eugene Bodichon, a Frenchman who had been in the colony for twenty years practicing medicine among the natives. They were married in London in 1857 and had dined with the Leweses before they left for a long tour of America before returning to their home in Africa. During the height of her agony over the Liggins story, Marian received the letter, excerpted below, from Algiers:

> My Darling Marian!
>
> Forgive me for being so very affectionate but I am so intensely delighted at your success. . . . I can't tell you how I triumphed in the triumph you have made. . . . There are some weeks passed since in an obscure paper I saw the 1st review and read one long extract which instantly made me internally exclaim that is written by Marian Evans, there is her great big head and heart and her wise wide views. . . . Now the more I get of the book the more certain I am, not because it is like what you have written before but because it is like what I see in you. . . . Very few things could have given me so much pleasure.
>
> 1st. That a woman should write a wise and *humourous* book which should take a place by Thackeray.
>
> 2nd. That you *that you* whom they spit at should do it! . . . Everybody (but Bessie and [my husband]) have bullied me for saying "My friend Marian" so you see I may take a little pet bit of delight to myself that you will be what all will wish to claim as "my friend Marian"! . . . This is only to tell you how I rejoice with you.

The letter thrilled Marian, who wrote, "God bless you, dearest Barbara, for your love and sympathy." George, too, was delighted. He added a note to Marian's reply: "You're a darling, and I have always said so. . . . But, dear Barbara, you must not call her Marian Evans again: that individual is extinct, rolled up, mashed, absorbed in the Lewesian magnificence."

Barbara did point to a problem that was obviously bothering Blackwood. George Eliot had written two books with deep moral overtones, and yet the real George Eliot was a woman who was indeed spit upon by most of that small part of society that knew anything about her. There were many among the book-buying public who would not read the works of an immoral woman. Critics who had praised the books would turn against them. Blackwood urged her to keep her secret, but contributions were still being collected for George Eliot the imposter.

Six months after the publication of *Adam Bede,* Marian met Sara Hennell and Cara and Charles Bray in London. This was the first time

Marian had seen Cara in the five years since her elopement. She revealed herself as George Eliot to the overwhelming surprise of all three of them. From then on, she and George began to quietly tell a few friends of her authorship. She wrote to Charles Dickens. He replied enthusiastically.

Blackwood had been right in his original assessment of what would happen once George Eliot's identity was no longer a secret. The *Athenaeum* published a beastly attack on *Adam Bede* and its author and suggested that she had set up Liggins for cheap publicity purposes. George usually protected her from all unfavorable comments but she somehow read this review, which left her stunned and ill.

The move to Holly Lodge had been a mistake. The new house was inconveniently distant from London and a house involved her in all of the hateful housekeeping duties which she had avoided as long as they lived in lodgings. Furthermore, the house was too close to other houses and the road, and she felt exposed in it. This feeling of exposure probably had more to do with what was being written about the real George Eliot than with the house itself, but she was not happy there. The Leweses soon became close friends of their neighbors the Richard Congreves. Nevertheless, Marian felt abandoned.

Her unhappiness was compounded by the death of Chrissey. Ill with consumption, Chrissey disobeyed Isaac and wrote to her sister to say that she was sorry she had ever quit writing. "It will be the greatest comfort I can possibly receive to know you are well and happy." Marian answered immediately. She wanted to visit her sister but Chrissey's daughter felt that the excitement would be too much for her mother.

In spite of her distress Marian continued to write. In April she finished a short story entitled *The Lifted Veil.* (It was published in the July issue of *Blackwood's Magazine.*) The next day she was at work on the book that was to become *The Mill on the Floss.*

In July the Lewes made a quick trip to Switzerland. The Congreves were in Lucerne, and Marian stayed with them while George went on to visit his boys. All three of them were at the Hofwyl School at that time. He had determined beforehand to tell his sons about his domestic relations. Marian sent a gift to each of the boys: a watch for Charles, a novel for Thornton, and a knife for Herbert. After dinner on the day of his arrival, father and sons went for a walk in the woods where he told them that his marriage to their mother was over and that he had been living for some time with the author of *Adam Bede.* "They were less distressed than I had anticipated and were delighted to hear about Marian," he confided to his journal. He stayed for three days, discussing future plans, listening to Charles play the piano, and taking long walks.

Marian and George had been back at Holly Lodge for a few days when Pug arrived. Blackwood had heard Marian say that she wished some nobleman would admire *Adam Bede* so much that he would send her a pug. He commissioned his cousin, a sportsman, to find a purebred dog for her. It was no easy task, but at last a suitable puppy was located, purchased at a high price, and delivered. The tiny short-haired dog with the pushed-in face and curly tail arrived on July 30. In thanking Blackwood, Marian wrote, "I see already that he is without envy, hatred, or malice—that he will betray no secrets, and feel neither pain at my success nor pleasure at my chagrin."

"He comes as a substitute for lost friends," she wrote to Cara. Pug was indeed a comfort. He was also a source of endless amusement. Although Lewes hinted that Pug was a bit short on brain power, he told Blackwood that he had "developed an aristocratic audacity and refinement since his introduction into literary society. He makes us shout with laughter continually."

Pug—his name as well as his breed—enlivened their lives for several years. His end is unknown. The next dog in the Lewes household was a bullterrier named Ben. Just as Marian portrayed children respectfully and unsentimentally in her novels, so she portrayed dogs. They are dignified and devoted and completely doglike.

In spite of Blackwood's kind gift, relations between him and his author grew strained. Marian was being courted by other publishers. Dickens was the owner of the publication *All the Year Round.* His *Tale of Two Cities* was running serially in the magazine. It would be followed by *The Woman in White* by Wilkie Collins. Then he wanted to run George Eliot's new novel. His agent told Lewes that he was prepared to top any offer made by Blackwood.

Blackwood, however, had given his author far more than was called for in the original agreement. Most novelists today receive 10 percent of the retail price of every book sold. Blackwood gave George Eliot one-third of the price of her books. She did not seem to him to be suitably grateful.

She, on the other hand, was upset by his reluctance to reveal her authorship. She also felt that he was less than totally enthusiastic about her new book. After a series of cool letters, Blackwood wrote very frankly of his position and she answered, equally frankly. In December he went to Holly Lodge and she gave him the first part of the new manuscript. Following the meeting, Blackwood wrote the Major that he had a pleasant meeting with the Leweses and that they had accepted his offer. "She is a fine character—all my former good opinion of her is restored. I am sure I cannot be mistaken both in her language and the expression of her face."

In the meantime, *Adam Bede* was continuing to gather readers and royalties. Queen Victoria was so taken with the novel that she commissioned a painter to illustrate two scenes from it. The paintings are in Buckingham Palace. By the end of its first year, *Adam* had earned over seventeen hundred pounds, this for an author who only a decade before had lived for most of a year on the one hundred pounds left her by her father.

George Lewes was also busy. If he had done nothing with the rest of his life but encourage George Eliot and act as her agent he would have made a valuable contribution. He did much more. His earnings never again approached hers, but he was both prolific and scholarly. He was a self-made scientist, not just a writer on scientific subjects. One of the highlights of this period for him was the acquisition of a new powerful microscope. His *Seaside Studies,* published in 1858, was followed by *Physiology of Common Life* in 1859, a book which became a text for medical students. In addition he wrote articles—some light, some serious—for a number of different publications.

It was Blackwood's custom to have Marian's handwritten manuscripts bound. He kept the manuscript for *Scenes* but he returned *Adam Bede* to her. She, in turn, gave it to George with this inscription: "To my dear husband, George Henry Lewes, I give this m.s. of a work which would never have been written but for the happiness which his love has conferred on my life."

The Mill on the Floss was completed in April 1860. The reviews were mixed. Some liked it better than *Adam Bede,* some less well. Sales were fantastic, greater than *Adam.*

The most distinctive quality of *The Mill* is its vivid portrayal of childhood, an example of which is included in the second chapter of this book. The major criticism is that most of the action is crammed into the last half of the book, which comes to a whirlwind melodramatic finale.

The education of Maggie and Tom Tulliver ends abruptly when their goodhearted but unwise father loses everything in bankruptcy to Mr. Wakem. Tom becomes a grind whose only goal is to pay back his father's debts. He has no time or sympathy for his sister. He hates Philip Wakem, whom he had known at school. Philip is a sensitive young artist with a deformed body who adores Maggie. She feels admiration and pity for Philip which she confuses with love until she meets Stephen Guest, who has been courting cousin Lucy. Just as Tom achieves his goal, Maggie and Stephen take a foolish and scandalous trip down the river which completes the alienation between Maggie and her brother, between Maggie and almost everyone.

Did Isaac recognize himself as Tom? If so, could he have been unmoved by his sister's devotion to him during childhood? Perhaps he considered it his due. What then must he have thought of later passages when the grown-up Maggie begs Tom for understanding?

"You have been reproaching other people all your life; you have been always sure you yourself are right; it is because you have not a mind large enough to see that there is anything better than your own conduct and your own petty aims."

Like Tom, Isaac was insensitive. It is doubtful that he was able to see this passage and others like it as his sister's plea for his acceptance of her chosen life style.

Two weeks after *The Mill* was finished, the Leweses set out for a three-month tour of Italy. No longer was it necessary for them to seek cheap lodging. This time they traveled in style. In Florence George suggested that Savonarola, a monk martyred in the fifteenth century, would make an interesting subject for a novel. Marian agreed.

On their way back to England they stopped in Switzerland to pick up Charles, whose education was completed. The three of them then went to Geneva to visit the tiny artist d'Albert Durade and his wife, whom Marian had not seen for ten years although they had corresponded. D'Albert was translating *Adam Bede* into French. They returned to Holly Lodge on July 1.

The relationship that developed—and the speed with which it developed—between Marian and her stepsons seems almost miraculous to us who have been raised on such phrases as "wicked stepmother" and "alienated youth." She referred to the boys as "ours," not "his." Before Charles arrived she had written to d'Albert expressing the hope that her heart would be large enough for all the love that would be required of her. Soon after their return to England she wrote Charles Bray that she thought they were "quite peculiarly blest in the fact that this eldest lad seems the most entirely loveable human animal of seventeen and a half that I ever met with or heard of."

The generosity of Marian at age forty is not nearly as remarkable as the generosity of Charles. Whatever his doubts and fears might have been, he referred to her as "Mother" from the very beginning and was a loyal and loving son for the rest of her life. Their bonds of love were further strengthened by their mutual joy in music. Before his arrival, Marian had bought a new piano. After his arrival they spent happy hours playing duets.

Of first importance after their return was finding a career for Charles. They had thought of publishing, but Blackwood was discouraging. They then consulted Anthony Trollope, a prolific author of novels and a government employee with the post office. Trollope arranged for Charles to take an examination for an opening in his department. Charles passed the exam which both Marian and George helped him study for, won the position, and started work on August 15. For a time he commuted from Holly Lodge, which was inconveniently distant from London. Marian, whose own mother had sent her off to boarding school at the age of five, could have suggested that Charles take lodgings in the city. Instead, they all three decided to move. They went first to a furnished house to see if they could bear living in town. They decided that they could, and leased a house at 16 Blandford Square for three years, hoping that at the end of that time the boys would be on their own and they could move back to the country. In the meantime, the second son, Thornton, came home and then went on to Edinburgh to prepare for an exam for the Indian service.

As soon as they returned to the city, Marian's health deteriorated again. Nothing—not the love of husband and sons nor the success of her novels—could protect her from physical suffering when she felt herself to be ostracized by society. In reality, she was now being neglected by only half of society—the female half. The Leweses received visits from many prominent men. Few women, however, were willing to risk their reputations by calling on her or inviting her to their homes. The women who did come were ardent feminists—with the exception of Sara Hennell. One woman caller was Mrs. Peter Taylor, whom Marian had met years before at the Chapmans. Pathetically, Marian wrote that she could not return her calls, that she never made calls because she had no carriage and all the calls she would have to make would take up too much of her time. The truth was that she had no need of a carriage because she had almost no one to call on, no one who would receive her.

In spite of her suffering, Marian wrote *Silas Marner* in London during the fall of 1860 and the winter of 1861. Although her Italian story was brewing in her mind, she wrote to Blackwood that she had one more English story she wanted to write. Shorter than any of her other novels, *Silas Marner* is really a legend about redemption and retribution. It takes place in a "far-off time" when a weaver named Silas Marner flees from a city where he has been falsely accused of stealing funds from a narrow religious sect that had been the core of his life. He sets up his loom in a cottage beside an abandoned stone quarry near the isolated village of Raveloe. Working long hours and depriving himself of every amenity, he becomes a miser whose only joy is counting his slowly accumulating gold.

The squire of Raveloe has four sons, the eldest of whom, Godfrey, has a horrible secret. He has been married to a drug-addicted young woman in a distant town. The second son, Dunstan, takes full advantage of his knowledge of the secret by blackmailing his brother. Godfrey eventually buys his brother's silence with his last possession, his horse. Dunstan takes the horse to a market to sell, but the horse dies before the sale is completed. Walking home through fog and darkness, Dunstan passes the weaver's cottage, open and unoccupied. He steals the gold and disappears.

Silas is distraught. All he has lived for has gone. Within a short time, however, the gold is replaced by a golden-haired baby girl. The child had been carried to Raveloe by her desperate mother, who planned to claim her title as the wife of Godfrey. Overcome by opium, she freezes to death. The child toddles into the weaver's cottage. Such a dramatic event naturally is noticed by all the villagers. Godfrey recognizes the dead woman and child but does not claim them. Silas insists on keeping the baby, whom he names Eppie. His whole life now centers on the child. The villagers who had looked on the weaver with suspicion begin to smile on the old man and his child.

Eppie grows to womanhood enveloped in love. Godfrey has married his childhood sweetheart, with whom he has no children. When the quarry is at last drained, the bones of Dunstan and the gold of Silas are revealed. Godfrey, overcome with remorse, tells the whole sordid story to his wife and they decide to claim Eppie. Too late. No promise of wealth or station can induce her to leave Silas. As the adopted father tells the natural father, "When a man turns a blessing from his door, it falls to them as take it in."

Silas Marner was published in one volume on April 2. The first edition was sold out before publication day. It was both a critical and a financial success. Unfortunately, John Blackwood was robbed of the joy he would otherwise have felt at the book's acceptance by the death of his brother, Major Blackwood, just six days after the book's publication.

Marian's religious views were now mature. She looked back on her years of pious Evangelicalism with tolerance and regretted her years as an antagonistic heretic. Although she would never return to dogmatic Christianity, she was fascinated by the religious experience in all its varieties. She saw religion—and especially Christianity—as a means to the final goal, moral purity. In each of her first four books—as well as in all of her future novels—she wrote about the struggle for human goodness. One of her most vivid and sympathetic characters is the young squire who appears—under different names—in both *Adam Bede* and *Silas Marner.* Filled with good intentions he sins, and he and others pay heavily for his weakness. Far from scorning this young man, his creator loves and pities him. It was this understanding of human weakness that raised her art to the highest level.

❧ 14 ❧

WITH *Silas* off to the printers, Marian returned immediately to the historical romance that had been born in Florence the previous year. The new book, *Romola* (pronounced Rom'-o-la), was a total departure from anything she had done in the past and required months of research. Step one was a return visit to Florence where both Marian and Lewes literally buried themselves in the fifteenth century, trying to see the city as it had been four centuries earlier and investigating the life and mind of Savonarola, the Florentine monk and martyr who was to become one of the central figures in the novel.

Anthony Trollope's brother Thomas, also a novelist, lived in Florence. At his suggestion, Marian and Lewes went with him to visit two remote monasteries. Lewes was sick with a hacking cold. Much of the journey had to be made on foot and horseback. Never mind. The research must go on. They left at 7 A.M. on a Monday morning and traveled by carriage until mid-afternoon. The only event worth noting was that one of the carriage horses fell and cut his head so severely that they thought him dead. The poor horse eventually struggled to his feet and they went on.

From three in the afternoon until after six, the journey was more arduous. Marian started off on a pony. The two men walked. Occasionally Lewes changed places with his wife. When they finally arrived at the "delicious valley of Camoldoli," Lewes recorded in his journal, "we felt it worth any amount of fatigue." They were greeted warmly at the monastery, where one of the monks prepared a soothing potion for Lewes' cough. After supper Marian and George had to climb another mile to a cowhouse, the only accommodation available to women.

Tuesday they saw more of the monastery, Lewes from the inside, Marian from the outside. They went on toward another monastery. En route Marian's horse fell at the edge of a cliff. "She was neither hurt nor shaken," wrote Lewes. "I who saw her fall felt very sick and faint from the shock." They finally headed back toward Florence on Thursday in a pelting rain.

Back in England the research continued. Marian was ill and despairing. Even George, the optimist, worried that she would never actually begin to write. Time and again she considered giving up the whole idea. Still she continued to read about fifteenth-century Italy. John Blackwood came for a visit and urged her on. Major Blackwood's son William was beginning to take over his father's former position as right-hand man to John. John Blackwood wrote his nephew that Marian was studying her subject as it had never been studied before.

Finally on January 1, 1862, Marian picked up her pen to begin writing *Romola,* a project which took her eighteen months. Most of the book was written in London where she was seldom happy. The subject of the book and the fact that some of the characters had been living men made the book more difficult to write than the country novels which were based almost entirely on her memory and her imagination. As a result she was ill and gloomy. George Lewes did his best to cheer her and to keep her writing. It was no easy task.

Today's reader of *Romola* can only admire George Eliot for trying to change her literary pace, and regret that she was not more successful in her attempt. That she knew almost everything there is to know about fifteenth-century Florence is obvious—too obvious. The cast of characters is enormous and confusing. The wealth of detail about Florentine life is ponderous. The political plots are incomprehensibly complex.

Nevertheless, George Eliot created three magnificent characters—

one historical and two fictional. Savonarola, the Florentine monk who called Florence to righteousness and was thus a prophet of the Reformation, is portrayed with all his strengths and weaknesses. Romola is the beautiful daughter of a scholar. She, too, might have been revered as a scholar except that no man at that time could take female intelligence seriously. Her struggle is a private one—for moral purity. Her husband Tito is a charming and beautiful Greek scholar. His flaw is that he forever seeks the easy way, turning his back on unpleasant facts and responsibilities until, at last, he has committed the most blatant sins. In some respects Tito resembles the weak young squires in George Eliot's country novels except that for him there is no redemption.

Publishers could not know in advance of the weaknesses in George Eliot's new novel. George Smith, the editor of *Cornhill Magazine*, offered more for the book than had ever before been offered for a novel. He was at last successful in luring her away from Blackwood. *Romola* began running in *Cornhill* in July with illustrations by Frederic Leighton, one of his generation's most popular artists. George Lewes was also working for *Cornhill* as a consulting editor.

John Blackwood took his author's infidelity like the gentleman that he was. Both his nephew Willie and the firm's London representative were angry. John Blackwood was hurt, but he urged his associates to keep their grievances to themselves. "Quarrels, especially literary ones, are vulgar," he wrote. John Blackwood was never vulgar!

Robert Browning was among the few who were enthusiastic about the opening chapters of *Romola*. Others were more critical. Sara, always blunt, apparently referred to some adverse remarks about the book in a letter which Lewes was reading aloud to his wife at breakfast. Glancing ahead as he read, he noted the offending paragraph and skipped it. The letter was conveniently misplaced so that Marian never saw it. As Lewes explained in a private letter to Sara, "A thousand eulogies would not give her the slightest confidence, but one objection would increase her doubts. With regard to *Romola* she has all along resisted writing it on the ground that no one would be interested in it; but a general sense of its not being possibly popular would not be half so dispiriting to her as the knowledge that any particular reader did not like it."

Marian's doubts about the value of her novel were increased by other worries. Chief among these was Lewes' health. Never well, he was decidedly worse during 1861 and 1862. He was losing weight and was often unable to work. Although he remained cheerful, she was despondent. They took many short trips during this time, hoping that changes in scenery and climate would help him. Her letters are filled with reports on his health—he is better and worse and better again. The word "death" begins to appear frequently in her letters.

Then there were Lewes' sons. "We are up to our ears in Boydom and imperious parental duties," Marian wrote to Barbara. Charles did not receive an expected promotion. Anthony Trollope checked with friends at the post office and wrote Lewes a candid letter telling him that the boy was careless, slow, and inefficient. The news gave Lewes a bilious attack. A month later he discovered that Trollope's report was harsh. Charles was slow but well liked. Charles seemed to be well liked by everyone.

In the meantime Thornton was studying for an examination that would lead to a government job in India. He passed the first part of the test in the summer of 1862 but failed the second part. Rather than return to his studies, he announced that he was going to Poland to fight the Russians. Marian and George were appalled at the idea, knowing that he was the kind of boy who might go regardless of his father's wishes. Thornton was the son most like George, witty and charming with a wide range of interests and a literary bent. He and a co-author had already written a pamphlet on forged stamps and how to detect them.

Finally in October 1863, nineteen-year-old Thornton set out for Natal in South Africa. Barbara Bodichon had given Thornton letters of introduction to friends and officials in Africa. The voyage was great fun. Thornton edited a newspaper for his fellow passengers and acted in amateur comedies. Once arrived he scurried around the country, meeting people and exploring opportunities. He found a temporary job with a French trader. "I shall have to look after the wagon . . .

and keep the books, and for this shall get £3 a month. Won't that be glorious?" he wrote to his parents. "I would have gone willingly for nothing at all, as the shooting and butterfly catching will be quite enough payment. . . . When I come back, I shall . . . join some coffee planter, where I can learn the business, and get my board and lodging in return for my work."

Herbert (Bertie), the youngest son, had also returned from Switzerland and was in Scotland learning farming, an occupation entirely to his liking.

During the summer of 1863, Marian had finished *Romola,* Thornton had failed the Indian exam, and the Lewes family had moved into what was to be their permanent home, The Priory, set deep in a garden in the Regent's Park section of London. In November they gave a combined housewarming and coming-of-age party for Charles. When Bertie came home for the Christmas holidays they enjoyed evenings of whist and music. Another addition to the family scene was George Lewes's mother, who accepted Marian with good grace and was a frequent visitor in her son's home.

Saturday nights the Leweses held open house for their friends, who were welcome to drop by without special invitations. Herbert Spencer was a regular. So, too, was George Redford, a doctor and writer, who was also an excellent cellist. He left his cello at The Priory since most Saturday evenings included music. Robert Browning was also a frequent caller.

The year 1864 was a blank as far as Marian's literary career was concerned. She gave *Cornhill* a story, *Brother Jacob,* which had been written several years earlier. The gift was apparently made in recognition of the fact that *Romola* had been a financial loss for its publisher. Lewes had an idea for a play he thought his wife might write. She tried but gave it up. She read Spanish history with the vague idea of doing a dramatic piece. During the year Lewes gave up his association with *Cornhill.* They took many short trips and a long trip to Paris and Italy. Lewes was still unwell.

Charles became engaged to Gertrude Hill, a young woman four years older than he. Charles seemed too young to marry but George and Marian were pleased with his choice. The wedding took place in the spring of 1865.

During the winter of 1865 Marian wrote a long poem and two articles for the *Pall Mall Gazette*. In the spring she wrote two signed reviews for the first edition of the *Fortnightly Review,* which was being edited by Lewes.

Then, after two years of literary floundering, she began work on a new novel. *Felix Holt, the Radical* has been described as George Eliot's political novel. The action takes place just before and just after the first election following the passing of the Reform Bill of 1832, which expanded the voting rolls and gave representation to industrial regions that had been slighted or ignored in the past when government had been almost wholly in the hands of country squires and wealthy land-owners. Thirteen-year-old Mary Ann Evans had witnessed a riot during the voting in Nuneaton, a scene which is a focal point of *Felix Holt.* The title character is an altruistic young man determined to cast his lot among working men. He is accused of manslaughter and leading the election-day riot. One of the candidates is a wealthy landowner named Harold Transome who has returned from fifteen years in the East to rebuild his family's ruined estates. He loses the election and almost loses the estate when he discovers that the legal heir may be a young girl who has been raised in poverty as the daughter of a dissident minister. The girl, Esther Lyon, is torn between duty and delight until she discovers that what she has looked on as delight may be less attractive than duty.

George Eliot returned to the firm of Blackwood and Sons with *Felix Holt.* The novel had already been rejected by *Cornhill* but John Blackwood never knew that. He greeted the first chapters of the new novel with his usual enthusiasm and offered her five thousand pounds. It was finished on May 31 and published on June 15, 1866. Three thousand copies were sold in the first three days.

The speed with which George Eliot's books were published seems miraculous today, when the publication of most books takes at least six months and frequently much longer. Sections of the George Eliot novels were set into type as they were received in Scotland. One reason for this speed was that until they were set into type there were no copies of her original handwritten manuscripts. If a manuscript were to be lost or burned before it had been set, it would be gone forever. The few and minor revisions were made on the proof sheets drawn from the type. One of the author's most reasonable worries was that a part of a manuscript would be lost in the mail. Once when she was going to Europe she even put an unfinished manuscript in a bank vault for safekeeping until her return.

As soon as *Felix Holt* was finished, the Leweses set out for two months in Europe. They returned to be immersed in family activities. Thornton had obtained a land grant in Africa and asked Bertie to come to help him farm the land. George and Marian outfitted Bertie for the trip and sent Thornton money to buy stock for his farm. All of Marian's money was placed in an account in George Lewes' name. She had by this time earned more than enough money to keep her comfortably for the rest of her life. Although she was always interested in pennies— her letters often refer to the cost of hotel rooms, etc.—she was extremely generous with large amounts. Bertie steamed out of England on September 9.

On September 24, the first child of Charles and Gertrude died at birth. Marian's affection for Gertrude had grown into a deep love. "She is so precious to us," Marian wrote to Sara soon after the baby's death. "Sometimes it requires an effort to feel affectionately toward those who are bound to us by ties of family, but it is as easy to me to love Gertrude as it is to love the clear air."

Several years earlier Marian had started a Spanish drama. She now returned to her studies of Spain with a different goal. By December Lewes' health was so miserable that he quit the *Fortnightly Review* and they headed south. After several weeks in Biarritz in southern France they decided to venture across the border into Spain, a dream of Marian's which she had feared would be too difficult for George. His health improved, however, and they spent hours in France studying Spanish, taking a dictionary with them on all of their walks and quizzing one another. The trip into Spain delighted them in every way, and they returned to England on March 16 with Lewes' health restored, if only temporarily.

Within a matter of days she announced her new project to John Blackwood. "The work connected with Spain is not a Romance. It is —prepare your fortitude—it is—a poem." She recognized from the beginning that this was not a work which would be financially profitable but she worked at it for more than a year. Payment was to be based on the number of copies sold, and Blackwood, who would surely have preferred to have his best-selling author at work on a popular novel, encouraged her every step of the way. So, too, did George, although his eyes were wide open to the problems of selling poetry. He wrote a private note to Blackwood warning him against printing too many copies.

George Eliot never in her life wrote a potboiler—a book written with no other aim than to make money. She wrote to please herself. That she made a great deal of money while doing so is almost incidental. "Don't you imagine how the people who consider writing simply as a money-getting profession will despise me for choosing a work by which I could only get hundreds where for a novel I get thousands?" she wrote to Cara. "I cannot help asking you to admire what my husband is, compared with many possible husbands—I mean, in urging me to produce a poem rather than anything in a worldly sense more profitable."

The Spanish Gypsy was inspired by a small painting of the Annunciation by Titian. In the painting Marian saw a young girl, the Virgin Mary, who was expecting to marry and lead a quite ordinary life. Instead she is told that because of her heredity she has been chosen for a great destiny, to be the mother of the Messiah. Marian felt that this simple story had in it all of the elements of great drama. She used the same set of circumstances set in a different time and place for her book-length narrative poem. A young Spanish girl has been raised as a noblewoman only to discover that she is destined by birth to be the leader of the gypsies.

Published on May 25, 1868, the book sold very well for poetry and was a critical success. One reviewer called it the greatest poem ever written by a woman—this within a few years of the death of Elizabeth Barrett Browning.

The composition of *The Spanish Gypsy* had been interrupted when she wrote the opening article for the January 1868 issue of *Blackwood's Magazine,* "Address to Working Men by Felix Holt." The occasion was the passage of the second reform bill which increased the voting rolls to include more middle-class workers and artisans. In this piece, Felix urges the newly enfranchised men to use their powers with restraint and wisdom.

During these years the Leweses' social life was expanding. Marian, however, was still extremely sensitive to criticism. She wrote to her old friends the Congreves that she could not go with them to some public place (probably a concert) while George was in Germany because people who saw her there would not know why he was absent. Did she still fear the gossips who had fourteen years earlier predicted that the alliance would not last?

In writing to Sara, she frequently seemed to be walking on eggs, always assuring her old friend of her love, always expressing great interest in Sara's work (a book entitled *Present Religion: As a Faith Owning Fellowship with Thought*) while seldom mentioning her own work.

To Cara, on the other hand, Marian revealed her real delight in their friendship and a certain lightheartedness. In writing to urge her to come to visit, she said that two professors were likely to come by during the evening, "but you will not mind that. They are Germans flavored with Sanskrit, not less interesting than the Orang and the Chimpanzee at the Zoological Gardens."

Through Barbara Bodichon, Marian was introduced to Emily Davies, who was trying to start a college for women, a project dear to Marian's heart. Once women had gained control over their own money, Marian had two other goals for women. One was the vote. The other was the opportunity for education. Still, she had reservations. All of her life she had been critical of "silly women novelists." Her fear was that women would try to fly too high. The greatest disgrace for a woman—or for a man—was to try to do work for which she was unfit, to do any work badly.

Although Marian was interested in women's rights and education, she was not an active feminist in the sense that she could have paraded in bloomers or even carried a sign demanding the vote. Her contribution was deeper and far more subtle. Her weapon was her pen. With it she demanded that women be recognized as first-class citizens capable of making decisions and acting with responsibility. The world was a better place because the young female preacher in *Adam Bede* did what was considered to be a man's work and did it well. Maggie would and could have helped Tom in the family crisis, but because she was a woman he would not even discuss his problems with her. Romola was a scholar, unrecognized as such simply because of her sex. In *Felix Holt,* old Mrs. Transome has been running her estates for years when her son comes home from the East to take over. He makes improvements in every area but without ever consulting her on anything more important than what color horses she wants to draw her new carriage. Completely oblivious to her as a person, he cannot understand why she is not thrilled with all that he has done for her. She agrees that he has been good to her, "—good as men are disposed to be to women, giving them cushions and carriages, and recommending them to enjoy themselves, and then expecting them to be contented under contempt and neglect."

The usual Victorian novel ended with wedding bells. Having achieved a good marriage, the heroine's life was complete. Not so, said George Eliot. In an age when birth control was considered immoral, she wept for the woman who gave birth year after year until her health was ruined. She cried out for the woman whose personality was submerged into that of her husband's, who was expected to be pretty and frivolous and to leave the problems of the world to men. No novelist ever drew more multi-dimensional women. They were George Eliot's contribution to the feminist cause.

BOOK IV

George Eliot
and
Mrs. Cross

⤠ 15 ⤟

MARIAN EVANS and George Lewes tramped through the fields of Surrey enveloped in grief. She loved autumn above all seasons and farmland above all terrains, but in October 1869 they offered small solace as she walked along with the face of dear Thornie ever before her.

The year 1869 should have been golden, marking her fiftieth birthday and her fifteenth year with Lewes. Indeed on New Year's Day she had been filled with hope. "A bright frosty morning! And we are both well," she recorded in her journal. "I have set myself many tasks for the year—I wonder how many will be accomplished?—A Novel called Middlemarch, a long poem . . . and several minor poems."

Within a matter of days, however, the first hint of grief arrived in a letter from South Africa. Thornie wrote that he was in great pain from a kidney stone. His father sent him money and urged him to hurry back to London. Although Marian was concerned about her stepson, her life went on as usual. During January and February she wrote two poems. "How Lisa Loved the King" was sent to John Blackwood for *Blackwood's Magazine.* After warning her that he would never give a fancy price for anything in the *Magazine* because he did not think that an article from one of the Apostles would much affect its sale, Blackwood offered her fifty pounds. A handsome offer which she accepted gratefully. Several months later, *Atlantic Monthly* in America offered her three hundred pounds for the second poem, "Agatha."

She also worked on the new novel and continued her reading and studies. On January 23 she recorded her activities in her journal: ". . . I have made a little way in constructing my new Tale, have been reading a little philology, have finished the 24th book of the Iliad, the first book of the 'Faery Queen,' Clough's poems, and a little about Etruscan things . . . Aloud to G. I have been reading some Italian, Ben Jonson's Alchemist and Volpone, and Bright's Speeches, which I am still reading—besides the first four cantos of Don Juan." Throughout her life, Marian's reading had been phenomenal; it was never diminished or lightened. She read in French, German, Greek, Latin, Italian, and Spanish—the classics and current fiction and nonfiction. She read to herself and aloud to George, obviously spending several hours each day with other people's books, even when she was writing a book of her own.

The Leweses' social life was ever expanding, and Sundays had replaced Saturdays as the time when friends were free to drop by. One who was invited for a Sunday afternoon was Charles Eliot Norton, a Bostonian with a wicked pen. The son of a Harvard professor and noted Unitarian minister, Norton arrived in London with his family in 1868 and moved into a house not far from The Priory. Lewes, who had met Norton through mutual friends, called to invite him and his wife to come on Sunday to meet Mrs. Lewes. As Norton wrote to an American journalist, he had never heard Mrs. Lewes spoken of with anything but respect. Nevertheless, the only women who called on her were women who were so emancipated that they didn't care what the world said about them or women who had no social position to maintain. The Nortons did not care to risk their reputations by visiting the Leweses.

Then Lewes invited them to lunch and they accepted readily. The turn-about-face may be accounted for by Norton's need to refuel his pen, a need which he placed above the need to protect his wife's reputation. Norton's report on the luncheon was venomous:

> Lewes received us at the door with characteristic animation; he looks and moves like an old-fashioned French barber or dancing-master, very

ugly, very vivacious, very entertaining. You expect to see him take up his fiddle and begin to play. . . . His acquirements are very wide, wider, perhaps, than deep, but the men who know most on special subjects speak with respect of his attainments. I have heard . . . Darwin . . . speak very highly of the thoroughness of his knowledge. . . . He has the vanity of a Frenchman; his moral perceptions are not acute . . . there is something in his air which reminds you of vulgarity.

Norton described The Priory as being pleasant and cheerful with well-filled bookshelves but "all the works of art in the house bore witness to the want of delicate artistic feeling, or good culture on the part of the occupants." With his pen well warmed by malicious comments on Lewes and his house, Norton drove in for the kill in describing Marian.

. . . One seldom sees a plainer woman; dull complexion, dull eye, heavy features. For the greater part of two or three hours she and I talked together. . . . She said not one memorable thing, but it was the talk of a person of strong mind who had thought much and who felt deeply, and consequently it was more than commonly interesting. . . . Her manner was too intense.

Finally, as if he wished to prove his own tolerance, Norton did report that "everyone who knows Mrs. Lewes well seemed attached to her, and those who know speak in the warmest terms of her relations to her husband and his family,—of her good sense and her goodness."

The Bostonians stayed until sunset but decided not to go back again, another decision to be quickly reversed. Within a matter of weeks they had not only returned to The Priory but had invited the Leweses to their home.

The Nortons were not the only Americans to show an interest in George Eliot. Harriet Beecher Stowe began a correspondence with Marian in 1869 which continued spasmodically for the rest of her life. The author of *Uncle Tom's Cabin* and *Dred* and the author of *Adam Bede* and *Silas Marner* wrote about their work and their families with the intimacy of two old friends.

In March the Leweses set out for two months on the Continent.

Three days after their return they called on Lewes' mother for a few hours. Thornie was waiting for them when they returned to The Priory. The sight of this twenty-five-year-old son was a shock. Although he was in good spirits he had lost fifty pounds and looked thin and worn.

The day after Thornie's return, a Sunday, must have been one of the worst days in the lives of either Marian or George. Thornie came downstairs in the morning but was soon in such pain that he was rolling in agony on the dining room floor. Lewes went out in search of an open pharmacy, a time-consuming task on a Sunday. While he was gone visitors arrived. Few of their friends knew that the Leweses were back from Europe, and they had been expecting no one on this first Sunday. But there, waiting to be entertained at the feet of the famous novelist, were three Americans: the malicious gossip's sister, Miss Grace Norton, Miss Sara Sedgwick, and a young man named Henry James. James was to become one of the great novelists of the late nineteenth and early twentieth centuries. (Future critics would claim that his art had been greatly influenced by George Eliot.) At this time, however, he was still seven years from his first novel. He had written some reviews, including three about George Eliot novels for American publications. Marian welcomed her guests and talked with them about her European trip. Finally James went to the dining room to see if he could do anything to help Thornie. When George finally returned with morphia to relieve his son's pain, James went out to summon the doctor. The Queen's own doctor, James Paget, came that evening.

The disease was tuberculosis of the spine, a painful and fatal disease which has become almost extinct in this age of antibiotics. For the next six months, George and Marian devoted hours of each day to the care and comfort of Thornton. They had a full-time nurse for him, and friends were kind. Barbara Borichon, in England at the time, came twice a week to visit the young man and sent him strawberries, grapes, and other treats. At least once—and perhaps more often—Thornie's own mother, Agnes, came to visit her son when Marian was away from the house.

Charles and his wife had been on vacation at the time of Thornie's return from Africa. When Charles finally saw his brother for the first time on June 1, he was so shocked at the sight of the wasted body that he fainted.

Thornie had good days and bad. During the good days his parents were filled with optimism. They even took several short trips. During the bad ones, as when his legs were completely paralyzed, they despaired.

Marian continued to try to work on her new novel but progress was slow. Her thoughts, instead of escaping from Thornie's pain to her novel, escaped for a time to her childhood days. Late in July she wrote the eleven Brother and Sister Sonnets. Completely unpretentious, the sonnets are simple evocations of her childhood and her love for Isaac:

> Long years have left their writing on my brow,
> But yet the freshness and the dew-fed beam
> Of those young mornings are about me now,
> When we two wandered toward the far-off stream.
>
> His years with others must the sweeter be
> For those brief days he spent in loving me.

Marian's loving heart is nowhere more completely revealed than in her ability to continue to love the brother who had turned away from her in stern judgment of the life she had chosen. That she longed for news of her family is evident in the letters she wrote to the son of her half-brother, Robert. The young man had begun the correspondence by writing to tell her of his father's death. She had continued it, asking about his mother and about her widowed half-sister, Fanny. We know, too, that Fanny and Isaac read and discussed the novels of their famous sister. We know it but she probably did not. The wall of silence was impenetrable.

Thornton Lewes died on October 19, 1869, in the arms of his stepmother. On that day, Marian wrote in her journal: "He was a sweet-natured boy—still a boy, though he had lived for twenty-five years and a half. . . . This death seems to me the beginning of our own."

The day after the funeral, Marian and George went to a farm south of London. They stayed several weeks, and eventually the deep calm of the countryside helped to restore their spirits.

❧ 16 ❧

"Mrs. Lewes is . . . writing, writing, writing—ye gods! How she is writing!" (George Lewes in 1872.) Picture her lying back in a reclining chair, her feet elevated, writing on a pad on her knees.

George Eliot began the decade with poetry. The poems of George Eliot have been dropped from most modern anthologies but they were greatly admired in their day. *Macmillan's Magazine* paid two hundred pounds each for "The Legend of Jubal" and "Armgart." American publishers paid another one hundred and fifty pounds for the two poems. Both were written in 1870, published, and forgotten.

But *Middlemarch* was also simmering toward the boiling point in that year. By the end of 1870 she had written one hundred pages of what was to become her greatest novel—some say the greatest novel ever written in English, others say one of the ten great novels of world literature. However it is judged, it is a masterpiece. Long, complex, and yet tidy, it contains numerous plots and subplots, scores of well-defined characters, a wealth of psychological insight, moments of tragedy, and hours of humor.

Basically, *Middlemarch* is a story of marriages, the expectations of young people in love and the reality of two people living together—in strength and joy or in misery and degradation. The novel opens with Dorothea Brooke, a young woman who longs for a noble purpose and expects to find it in marriage to an aging and ugly clergyman, Edward Casaubon. He has devoted his life to his "Key to all Mythologies," and Dorothea plans to help him with his work. It is only after marriage that she discovers that his scholarship is barren, that he is simply making outlines and rewriting paragraphs of a work that will never be completed. Even his parishioners have no need of her. Dorothea's sister Celia marries Sir James Chettam. Both are simple young people who live together contentedly with no greater purpose than raising beautiful babies and acting as kind landlords to their tenants. The idealistic young Dr. Lydgate sacrifices his dreams for Rosamond, whose beauty has blinded him to her shallowness. The marriages of people who have lived together for many years are also put under the microscope. *Middlemarch* deserves a "mature audiences only" rating, not because it contains sex scenes, acts of violence, or four-letter words, but because it takes maturity to appreciate its depth. Few teen-agers enjoy this book.

It is a long book—more than eight hundred pages in most editions —and Lewes and Blackwood devised a new plan for its publication. It was first released in eight bimonthly installments beginning in December 1871. The first installment was greeted with enthusiasm, and subsequent installments were awaited with impatience. Readers discussed and speculated on the fate of the characters. Marian did not know what the critics were saying about her creation—George read the reviews, favorable and unfavorable, and cut them out before she looked at the publications in which they appeared. Her only critics were her husband and her publisher, both of whom knew that the key to her production was unqualified praise. Still, she could not have been oblivious to the stir her book was creating. A judge told Barbara Bodichon that during the opening of the Dublin Exhibition he had noticed that the Archbishop's eyes never left the inside of his hat during all of the long speeches. The observer could only suppose that he was listening with rapt attention. The Archbishop was, in fact, reading an installment of *Middlemarch* which he had tucked into the hat.

During the months of writing, George handled most of his wife's correspondence and continued to work on his own *Problems of Life and Mind.* His was a large multi-volumed philosophical study which he frequently referred to as his "Key to All Mythologies." He referred to himself as Casaubon and to his wife as Dodo, Dorothea's nickname. This was done in jest, yet he told Blackwood that Dorothea "is more like her creator than anyone else and more so than any other of her creations." As soon as *Middlemarch* was finished, Marian turned her full attention to George's *Problems,* proofreading and editing his manuscript. The Leweses also took another trip to the Continent.

During the years 1870 to 1873, both Marian and George Lewes had been frequently ill. Although many of Marian's illnesses were imaginary, at least one during this period definitely was not. In the fall of 1871 she was confined to her room for four weeks, and when she was better she wrote Cara that she was as thin as a "medieval Christ."

Their illnesses did not prevent them from traveling far and often, but a permanent country retreat began to look more and more attractive to them. They could not find what they wanted to buy and so they rented a cottage or house in the country each summer. There had been a time when they had needed a sanctuary because Marian felt herself to be scorned and neglected in the city. Now they needed to escape to find peace from the "Lords and Ladies, poets and cabinet ministers, artists and men of science" whom George said were crowding in upon them. He was speaking the truth. Alfred Lord Tennyson was a near neighbor at one of their summer homes. They lunched with the Charles Darwins. Ivan Turgenev, the Russian novelist, visited them.

One family that greatly enriched their lives was the Cross family, widowed mother and nine children. Herbert Spencer had introduced Lewes to Mrs. Cross and her eldest daughter when the two men were on a walking tour in 1867. In 1869 in Rome, Marian and George Lewes met Mrs. Cross, her eldest daughter and son-in-law, and her son John Cross. This was the beginning of an affectionate relationship between the two families which lasted for the rest of their lives. They visited one another often, and the Leweses spent several Christmases at the Cross home in Weybridge. John Cross was a banker who took over the Lewes investments and managed them extraordinarily well. They soon began referring to him as their nephew.

Another new friend was Elma Stuart, a young craftswoman. She had come to adore the novels of George Eliot and made a hand-carved book slide which she sent to the author in care of Blackwood. From that time on Mrs. Stuart devoted much of her life to her "spiritual mother," as she referred to her idol, continually sending her gifts and writing and receiving letters.

Nor were old friends forgotten. The Brays had endured many financial crises. In 1873 Marian sent Cara fifty pounds with a delicately worded letter asking her to accept a commission to write a book that would teach children to be kind to animals. Cara demurred but finally kept the money and wrote the book. When no publisher could be found for it, Marian paid to have it printed. (Later Marian included Cara in her will with a bequest that would provide her friend with one hundred pounds a year for life.)

The Lewes family was also growing and prospering. Bertie married in South Africa. Blanche Southwood Lewes was born to Gertrude and Charles. No grandmother could have rejoiced more in the birth of a baby.

By the end of 1873, Marian was simmering toward another big book, *Daniel Deronda.* Less perfectly structured than *Middlemarch,* it nevertheless contains elements that make it one of her most interesting novels.

Blackwood called the heroine, Gwendolen Harleth, a fascinating witch. She is an arrogant, ambitious beauty who sells her soul to marry for wealth and power. She is both nasty and attractive. In her completeness as a living human being she is one of George Eliot's finest creations. By contrast, the title character, Daniel Deronda, seems bloodless. Almost too good to be believable, he has been raised as a well-educated young Englishman. His parentage, however, is a mystery. He is in love with two women, the tormented Gwendolen and a simple young Jew whom he has rescued from a suicide attempt.

What some readers considered to be the novel's greatest flaw and others its greatest strength is its Jewish element. Mary Ann Evans had first exhibited her interest in Judaism during her pious teen-age years when she had refused to attend the London theater with Isaac and had spent the evening alone in her room reading Josephus' *History of the Jews.* This interest grew while she was translating the Strauss book. In 1858 the Leweses had visited an old Jewish burial ground and synagogue in Prague, and their guide had read to them in Hebrew. Finally in 1866 she had met Emanuel Deutsch, a Hebrew scholar who was an assistant librarian at the British Museum. At the same time that he was writing an article on the Talmud for the *Quarterly Review,* Deutsch was visiting The Priory regularly and beginning to teach Marian Hebrew. In 1869 Deutsch visited Palestine and returned to England with a vision of a Jewish nation. Suffering from cancer, he withdrew from society. One of the few people whom he allowed to visit him was Marian Lewes. He died in 1873 but his ideas lived on to be expressed by the visionary young scholar Mordecai in *Daniel Deronda.*

One of George Eliot's most delightful qualities is her ability to laugh at the foibles of the English gentry. Her readers loved her humor and were charmed with the early chapters of the new novel. When she changed pace and introduced her cast of Jewish characters, most of whom are treated with such respect that they emerge as lifeless marble statues, her Christian readers were baffled and disappointed. Her Jewish readers were delighted.

Another fascinating element in *Daniel Deronda* is its feminist dimension. Daniel's mother eventually reveals herself to her son. She is a Jew who has turned her back on both her faith and her son in order to devote her life to her career. The very antithesis of the ideal of Victorian womanhood, Daniel's mother does not regret her decision, nor does she tearfully beg her son's forgiveness. She does try to explain her actions:

§ . . . Every woman is supposed to have the same set of motives or else to be a monster. I am not a monster, but I have not felt exactly what other women feel—or say they feel, for fear of being thought unlike others . . . I ought to say I felt about you as other women say they feel about their children. I did *not* feel that. I was glad to be freed from you. . . . You may try—but you can never imagine what it is to have a man's force of genius in you, and yet suffer the slavery of being a girl. To have a pattern cut out. . . . [My father was] a clever physician—and good: I don't deny that he was good. A man to be admired in a play. . . . But such men turn their wives and daughters into slaves. They would rule the world if they could; but not ruling the world, they throw all the weight of their will on the necks and souls of women. . . . §

Marian was truly ill during the writing of much of *Daniel Deronda.* Kidney stones, which were to plague her for the rest of her life, were first diagnosed in February 1874. In May she was in a state of extreme depression. She was always depressed while she was writing. In addition she was ill. A further contributor to her dark mood may have been Edith Griffiths, Isaac's daughter, who called with her husband, a clergy-man, in April. Edith brought photographs of Griff which her aunt pro-fessed joy at seeing. Marian had now had contact with two of her nieces—Edith and Chrissey's daughter Emily, whom she saw often—and her nephew Robert. But the pictures of Griff must have increased her longing for Isaac and Fanny. The Brother and Sister Sonnets had been included in *The Legend of Jubal and Other Poems,* which Blackwood published that year. Marian may have hoped that Isaac would be moved to acknowledge them. If so, she was disappointed.

The Lewes family, however, remained close. George's mother was dead but Charles lived near, and his little Blanche and her baby sister Maud gave great joy. Bertie fell ill and died in South Africa, leaving a young wife and two children, a little girl named Marian after her step-grandmother and an infant named George after his grandfather. Bertie's family was added to the roster of people supported by the Leweses, a list which also included his legal wife and his widowed sister-in-law and her son.

Still, the joy of Marian's life, and her all-in-all, was George Henry

Lewes. His love was one that she never took for granted, and his joy in promoting her books and her pleasure never faltered.

All social doors were now open to Mr. and Mrs. Lewes. In the summer of 1875 the Queen of Holland asked to have George Lewes presented to her at a garden party. "I admire your writing," the Queen said to George. "As to your wife's, all the world admires them." They were also invited to a party to meet the King of Belgium. Although Marian did not attend that party, she did attend a number of dinner parties and private musicals. The author of *Middlemarch* was now the star of any hostess' guest list.

Daniel Deronda was published during the summer of 1876, while the Leweses were in Switzerland and Germany. They returned to find the English reading public, from the working class to high society, ready to worship George Eliot.

At Westminster Abbey, where the Leweses were attending the wedding of Tennyson's younger son, a lady gazed devotedly at Marian and then quietly came up to stroke her cloak. After a concert a young woman helped her with her cloak and then kissed her hand and cheek. Surprised but always polite, Marian said, "Forgive me, but I don't recollect you."

"Oh! it is too good of you to let me," said the unknown worshiper. "If you speak to me I shall cry."

A woman wrote to tell George Eliot that the experiences of Gwendolen Harleth had saved her from a disastrous marriage. Women wrote to ask her advice on moral and religious matters. Others wrote just to say thank you.

Edith Simcox was one of several young women worshipers who became regular visitors at The Priory, encouraged by George in his continuing effort to strengthen his wife's self-confidence. Edith was a writer and social worker whose great cause became George Eliot. Like Alma Stuart, she was soon calling her idol "Mother." Unfortunately, Edith went overboard in her effusions, trying to kiss Marian's feet—which were pulled away—and filling her diary with words of love which are distasteful to post-Freudian moderns.

Even Victoria's royal daughters wanted to meet the famous author. The Princess Louise, a young sculptor who was interested in education for women, asked a liberal statesman, George Goschen, to invite the Leweses to dinner so that she might meet them. Etiquette demands that the commoner be presented to royalty, but on this occasion the Princess asked to be presented to the famous commoner. During dinner, conversation turned to women's suffrage.

"But you don't go in for the superiority of women, Mrs. Lewes," said the Princess.

"I think Mrs. Lewes rather teaches the inferiority of men," said Thomas Huxley, who was also present.

Not to be outdone by her younger sister, Victoria's eldest daughter, who was married to the Crown Prince of Germany, also asked the Goschens to invite the Leweses to a dinner they were attending. The Princess began the conversation with the commonplace "You know my sister Louise." The Prince begged the Leweses to let them know the next time they were in Berlin. There was only one blight on the evening. The Princess stood most of the evening so, of course, everyone else had to stand.

Another interesting dinner party was one of Sir Henry Thompson's famous Octaves. These were dinners of eight courses served at eight o'clock to eight guests.

In addition to their regular Sunday open houses, more and more friends called during the week, and the Leweses, too, gave small parties. At one of these Tennyson, England's poet laureate, read his verse novelette *Maud*. New friends included Richard Wagner, the great composer of operas, and his wife, who was the daughter of Liszt. The Leweses saw the Wagners often while they were in London.

With all the social life of London, the Leweses' need for a country retreat became ever more desperate. John Walter Cross, their financial advisor and "nephew," found just the place for them late in 1876. It was The Heights in Surrey, deep in the country and yet convenient to the city. Lewes described it as "not a bad version of Paradise before the serpents (visitors) spoiled the garden." The Leweses spent two long summers, 1877 and 1878, in their "Eden."

Meanwhile, all of the books continued to sell. In 1876 Marian wrote John Blackwood a letter of appreciation which brought tears to his eyes and which he valued so highly that he put it in a safe place for his grandchildren. Most of the George Eliot-Blackwood correspondence survived in the Blackwood files—letters about printing schedules, bindings, and other trivia. This special letter was lost.

John Blackwood was hoping for another great novel. "We have a long career of successive triumphs to look back upon and I hope there is much yet before us," he wrote. George Eliot gave no indication that she was even thinking of another novel. She did send him an old manuscript, a poem called "A College Breakfast Party." He did not think it suitable for the readers of his magazine but it was eventually sold to *Macmillan's*.

George Lewes was the producing author during this period. He was hard at work on the fourth volume of his *Problems of Life and Mind*. His work was interrupted by illness. During the summer of 1878 Blackwood urged the Leweses to visit him and his family at their country home near the golf links of Saint Andrews. They wanted to go, but Lewes' lack of health made the trip impossible. George wrote that he could no longer work at all, that he couldn't even read for more than an hour. Even listening to his wife reading aloud soon wearied him.

There was a second invalid at The Heights that summer. She was Elinor, Charles' third daughter, who had been sent to the country with her nurse. The baby recovered quickly. In a long, loving letter to Maud, who had just passed her fourth birthday, Marian wrote that the baby's cheeks were pink and she was looking stronger. In the same letter she described The Heights.

> . . . There are a great many tall trees all around us, and sometimes there are squirrels with bushy tails running up them so fast that you could hardly catch sight of them. There are little snakes in the cucumber bed. They like to be there, because it keeps them warm. Last year there were a great many moles, which are little black creatures with tiny white hands, and with these hands they scratch themselves holes for a long way under the ground, and throw out the

earth in little hills above them. That spoils the grass, but the moles do not mean to be naughty. They are only working very hard to make themselves houses. . . .

After months of literary idleness, George Eliot had begun work that summer. She wrote a series of essays which George sent off to Blackwood on November 21, one week after they had returned to The Priory. In his note to Blackwood, he reported that he was better. He was not. Within the week, Marian had written to Blackwood to say that she could do nothing about the new book while her husband was ill. She also wrote Barbara: "I have a deep sense of change within, and of a permanently closer companionship with death."

George Henry Lewes died on November 30, 1878. His wife of twenty-four-and-a-half years went into seclusion.

❧ 17 ❧

"HERE I and sorrow sit," Marian wrote in her diary on January 1, 1879. Except for Charles, she sat alone. She had not attended her husband's funeral. She could not even read the letters of condolence that came from all over Europe. But she was not idle. She had a great goal, the completion of the fourth volume of *Problems of Life and Mind,* and she put all her feeble energy into that project.

When she was at last able to write a few letters, they were addressed to her closest friends. "I bless you for all your goodness to me," she wrote to Barbara Bodichon, "but I am a bruised creature, and shrink even from the tenderest touch. As soon as I feel able to see anybody I will see you. . . ." To John Cross she wrote, "Sometime, if I live, I shall be able to see you—perhaps sooner than anyone else—but not yet."

She could not remain cloistered forever. There was business to attend to. All of the money she and George had earned and both of their homes were in his name. In his will he had left his copyrights to Charles. Everything else was left to "Mary Ann Evans, spinster." That phrase, which was surely a legal necessity, could not have failed to hurt her. Nevertheless, she had to sign the papers that would transfer the property to her. She needed money. There were all of the Lewes dependents to be provided for—his legal wife, Agnes; Bertie's widow and children; Lewes' sister-in-law and her son. These relatives received a total of about five hundred pounds a year. In addition she needed five thousand pounds with which to establish the George Henry Lewes Studentship, her memorial to her husband. The Studentship provided financial aid to young scientists—male or female—who needed support to continue research in physiology.

As winter turned into spring she began to force herself back into the world. On February 23 she saw John Cross for the first time and saw him often from that time on. They had grief in common—John's mother, to whom he had been unusually close, had died the week after George. Marian began to go out in her carriage and to see her closest friends.

She corrected the printed proofs of her book *Impressions of Theophrastus Such.* The single volume was published in May with a statement by Blackwood noting that the essays had all been written the previous year—before Lewes' death. The *Impressions* are a series of interconnected essays, presumably the autobiographical reminiscences of an old bachelor named Theophrastus Such. Somewhat ponderous, they nevertheless contain such George Eliot witticisms as this: "Blessed is the man who, having nothing to say, abstains from giving in words evidence of the fact." The last volume of *Problems of Life and Mind* was published in December.

In the meantime, Bertie's widow, Eliza, and her two children had arrived from Africa. Eliza seems to have expected that she would be welcomed into the home of her famous and wealthy stepmother-in-law. She was not. Charles took her and her children into his home for a time and then helped them find schools and lodging. Marian loved Charles and his wife and daughters deeply. She did not feel the same warmth toward Eliza and her children. On her part, Eliza seems to have been discontented and troublesome. It was not long before Marian was hoping that Eliza would take her children and return to her own family in Natal.

In spite of her personal problems, ill health, and grief, Marian was beginning to find some pleasures in her life. She was seeing more and more of John Cross, with whom she had begun to read Dante's *Inferno* in Italian. She moved to The Heights for the summer, and when Cross was at his family's country house a few miles away he came to visit her almost every day. There he encouraged her to play the piano again. In September, Barbara Bodichon came to spend three days with her.

Fall brought another grief—the death of her publisher, John Black-wood. On November 1 she resumed her life at The Priory. On Novem-mer 29 she noted the anniversary of Lewes' death in her diary. She had read all his letters on that day and packed them together to be buried with her. She also copied out a long poem by Emily Brontë entitled "Remembrance." Following are the first and fifth verses:

> Cold in the earth, and the deep snow piled above thee!
> Far, far removed, cold in the dreary grave!
> Have I forgot, my only Love, to love thee,
> Severed at last by Time's all-wearing wave?
>
> No other sun has lightened up my heaven,
> No other star has even shone for me;
> All my life's bliss from thy dear life was given,
> All my life's bliss is in the grave with thee.

∾ 18 ∾

On May 6, 1880, Marian Evans married John Walter Cross. It was a small church service with Charles Lewes giving "his mother" away. The only guests were the groom's brothers and sisters and their spouses. London gossips were thrilled!

The bride was sixty years old; the groom was forty. Instances of older women marrying young men were rare but not unheard of. Three years earlier Marian had written Barbara Bodichon about the marriage of Thackeray's daughter Anne, age forty, to a young man of twenty-three. Marian wrote that she had recently known several instances where young men, even young men with "brilliant advantages" had chosen women whose attractions were "wholly on the spiritual order."

Some were critical of the marriage because they had misunderstood Marian's relationship with George Lewes. Having interpreted that relationship as a protest against convention, they were dismayed at what they saw as a betrayal of the concept of free love.

Others were critical because the marriage took place so soon after the death of George Lewes. They did not realize that the marriage was based on mutual need. Her companionship and the hours they spent reading together had helped fill the void left in John Cross' life when his mother had died. There is little doubt that she was something of a mother figure to him. As for her, the mature and successful author was no different from the passionate young girl in her need for some one person to be her all-in-all. She was not fit to stand alone. He was enthusiastic about her work. He even admired *Romola,* the novel that many criticized but which was one of her own favorites. Furthermore he had been a close friend to both her and George Lewes, had managed their investments, and was perfectly capable of advising her on all business matters. Then there was the added attraction of his brothers and sisters. They had loved her as "aunt"; they welcomed her as "sister." In response to a letter from Eleanor Cross, Marian wrote, "You can hardly think how sweet the name Sister is to me, that I have not been called by for so many, many years."

The day before the wedding Marian wrote to a few old friends so that they would receive the news on her wedding day and not from the newspapers. In each case she pointed out how John Cross had been loved and trusted by George Lewes. She told her friends that she would continue to provide for the Lewes family. Fearing that there were those who would say that he was marrying her for her money, she also took pains to point out that Cross had a sufficient fortune of his own. Her friends responded graciously.

Isaac, conventional to the end, was delighted that his sister was at last legally married. Soon after George's death, Isaac's wife had written a letter of sympathy. Now at last Isaac himself wrote: "My dear sister/ I have much pleasure in availing myself of the present opportunity to break the long silence which has existed between us, by offering our united and sincere congratulations to you and Mr. Cross. . . ."

Marian and John left for Italy right after the wedding. Isaac's letter was forwarded to Milan. Her response was effusive: ". . . it was a great joy to me to have your kind words of sympathy, for our long silence has never broken the affection for you which began when we were little ones. . . ." She also wrote about his family in a way that demonstrated her interest. She had heard from Chrissey's daughter that his wife had been ill. Friends had admired the sermons of his son Frederick, a clergyman. She had seen his daughter Edith, "a noble-looking woman."

Fanny did not write. Always sensitive, she may have felt that a letter now, after so many years of silence, would be unacceptable.

The wedding trip rejuvenated Marian. She was animated and enthusiastic. Above all, she was healthy! Not that her love for John Cross could ever replace her love for George Lewes. Her attitude toward this December marriage was summed up in a letter she wrote to Charles from Switzerland. "I had but one regret in seeing the sublime beauty at the Grande Chartreuse. It was, that the Pater had not seen it. I would still give up my own life willingly if he could have the happiness instead of me. But marriage has seemed to restore me to my old self. I was getting hard, and if I had decided differently I think I should have become very selfish. To feel daily the loveliness of a nature close to me, and to be grateful to it, is the fountain of tenderness and strength to endure."

John's response to the marriage is more difficult to assess. He undoubtedly worshiped his famous wife. The first part of the wedding trip was delightful. Then on June 16 in Venice, something happened to him. He was definitely ill, perhaps with typhoid fever, perhaps with a mental derangement. There are those who believe that he jumped from the balcony of his hotel into the Grand Canal in a suicide attempt. Whatever happened, his older brother William Cross rushed from England to Venice. After a short time the three of them started homeward through Germany. William left them after a few weeks and the bride and groom continued on alone, arriving at The Heights on July 26.

During the summer John's health was restored. He made frequent trips to the city to attend to his banking business and to oversee the preparations at the Chelsea house which would be their home in the fall. He played lawn tennis and chopped down large trees at The Heights to improve the view. He and his wife also made family visits.

Marian's health deteriorated. The kidney disorder returned with a vengeance. She was in bed for a week during the summer and ailing for a long time after.

On December 3 they moved to the house on Cheyne Walk in Chelsea, described as beautiful, with a view of the river. On Friday, December

17, they went to see *Agamemnon* performed in Greek by Oxford under-graduates. They enjoyed it so much that Marian proposed that she and her husband should devote part of the winter to reading Greek drama together. The next afternoon they attended a concert at St. James Hall, and in the evening she played through some of the music they had heard at the concert. Sunday Herbert Spencer and Edith Simcox called on the Crosses. Marian had a slight sore throat. Monday it was worse and the doctor was called in. Wednesday evening she died.

Her husband, Herbert Spencer, and a few others wanted her to be buried in the poet's corner of Westminster Abbey—the burial site of Chaucer, Dickens, and others. Letters were written on her behalf to the dean of the Abbey by a number of prominent men. Huxley, however, advised that the project be dropped before opposition forces could turn the proposed burial into a scandalous debate. Westminster Abbey is a Christian church devoted to faith in the divinity of Jesus Christ, a faith which Marian had denied. Her husband, therefore, chose a grave site for her that was as near to George Lewes' grave as possible.

The funeral took place on December 29, a bitterly cold winter day. The chief mourners were her husband, John Cross; her "son," Charles Lewes; and her brother, Isaac Evans, whom she had not seen in twenty-seven years. They were joined by a throng of famous men—Herbert Spencer, Robert Browning, George DuMaurier, Thomas Huxley, William Blackwood—and an even larger throng of unknown admirers. The service was conducted by a Unitarian minister using much of the service from the traditional Book of Common Prayer.

O May I Join the Choir Invisible

O May I join the choir invisible
Of those immortal dead who live again
In minds made better by their presence: live
In pulses stirred to generosity,
In deeds of daring rectitude, in scorn
For miserable aims that end with self,

In thoughts sublime that pierce the night like stars,
And with their mild persistence urge man's search
To vaster issues . . .

      This is life to come,
Which martyred men have made more glorious
For us who strive to follow. May I reach
That purest heaven, be to other souls
The cup of strength in some great agony,
Enkindle generous ardor, feed pure love,
Beget the smiles that have no cruelty,
Be the sweet presence of a good diffused,
And in diffusion ever more intense.
So shall I join the choir invisible
Whose music is the gladness of the world.

                  —George Eliot

✌ AUTHOR'S NOTE ✌

George Eliot was afraid of biographers. She never cooperated with any of the journalists who wished to write about her. She destroyed most of the letters she received. Those from George Henry Lewes were buried with her.

Her fear was not unfounded. The few contemporary biographical notes written about her were mostly wrong—her father was a poor clergyman, she had been tutored by Herbert Spencer, etc. Furthermore, she was distressed by the trivia written about Charles Dickens soon after his death. She felt that a writer should be judged by his books and not by the details of his personal life.

When the clamoring for information about the woman who called herself George Eliot would not be stilled, her husband, John Walter Cross, decided to prepare her biography himself. His *George Eliot's Life as related in her Letters and Journals* was published by Blackwood in three volumes in 1885. The first chapter of this work is a sketch of her childhood written by Mr. Cross. The rest of it consists of excerpts from her correspondence and diaries with explanatory notes by Mr. Cross. Charles Lewes, Isaac Evans, William Blackwood, and many other friends cooperated with Mr. Cross. Unfortunately but understandably, Mr. Cross wished to offend no one, least of all the memory of the woman he worshiped. She emerges from the pages of his biography as always wise and loving but never frivolous. He eliminated the sentence in her letter to Cara in which she said she was "as thin as a medieval Christ." There is no mention of her estrangement from Isaac, no hint of her difficulties in the Chapman household. When the book was finally published Gladstone referred to it as "a Reticence in three volumes."

Several of her contemporaries wrote reminiscences of her, but it was left to Gordon Haight, a professor of English at Yale, to do the detective work that was to reveal the real George Eliot. In 1933 he began to search out and to study her correspondence. He edited *The George Eliot Letters* published by Yale University Press in 1954. He then wrote *George Eliot: A Biography,* published by the Oxford University Press in 1968. I urge anyone who wishes to examine George Eliot's life in greater detail to read Mr. Haight's *Biography.* It is both scholarly and readable.

In preparing my much shorter biography, I have relied heavily on the correspondence collected in *The George Eliot Letters.* Unless otherwise noted below, the quotations may be found within the seven volumes of this work.

In Chapter 3 I have used excerpts from an early essay and novel. They are from a school notebook added to the George Eliot Collection at Yale in 1961 and printed for the first time in the Appendix to *George Eliot: A Biography* by Mr. Haight.

In Chapter 3 I have also quoted from Mr. Cross's "Introductory Sketch of Childhood," from his book *George Eliot's Life.* The review of the English translation of the Strauss book in Chapter 7 first appeared in *The Prospective* and was quoted in the Cross *Life.* The description of the passage to Belgium in Chapter 10 and the Goethe quotation in Chapter 11 are also from the Cross *Life.* When she wrote "Here I and sorrow sit," in her journal, she was quoting Shakespeare's *King John.* This quotation appears in the Cross *Life* and in Chapter 17 of this book.

I have imagined George Eliot's thoughts in three short passages. The first is in Chapter 1 when she is leaving home. The second is in Chapter

10 when she is eloping. The third is in Chapter 15 when she is grieving for Thornton. All three of these passages are based on facts revealed in her letters and journals.

I have also used many selections from George Eliot's published works.

It is my hope that readers of this book will have become interested in the novels; it is they by which George Eliot wished to be judged. Her books of fiction are listed below with the dates of their original publication.

Scenes of Clerical Life, 1858
Adam Bede, 1859
The Mill on the Floss, 1860
Silas Marner, 1861
Romola, 1863
Felix Holt, 1866
Middlemarch, 1872
Daniel Deronda, 1876

—LouAnn Gaeddert, 1976

~ INDEX ~

3 1181 00523 3383

SALT LAKE

SALT LAKE COUNTY
LIBRARY SYSTEM

RIVERTON BRANCH

Y92
Eli   Gaeddert, L.   **61801**
             All-in-all
c1976   7.95

**PLEASE BRING ME BACK ON TIME
WITH THE DATE DUE CARD IN MY
POCKET.***

*Sorry, I must charge for all lost
or damaged cards.

SALT LAKE COUNTY
LIBRARY SYSTEM